Volume II
The Roaring Twenties and an Unsettled Peace
(1919–1929)

The Twentieth Century

The Progressive Era and
the First World War
(1900–1918)

The Roaring Twenties and
an Unsettled Peace
(1919–1929)

The Great Depression
and World War II
(1930–1945)

Postwar Prosperity
and the Cold War
(1946–1963)

The Civil Rights Movement
and the Vietnam Era
(1964–1975)

Baby Boomers and the
New Conservatism
(1976–1991)

Volume II
The Roaring Twenties and an Unsettled Peace
(1919–1929)

Editorial Consultants

Matthew T. Downey, University of California at Berkeley
Harvey Green, Northeastern University
David M. Katzman, University of Kansas
Ruth Jacknow Markowitz, SUNY College at Oswego
Albert E. Moyer, Virginia Polytechnic Institute

Macmillan Publishing Company
New York
Maxwell Macmillan Canada
Toronto

Editorial Credits

Developed and produced by Visual Education Corporation, Princeton, N.J.

Project Editor: Richard Bohlander

Associate Project Editor: Michael Gee

Writers: Linda Barrett, Cathie Cush, Galen Guengerich, Lois Markham, Donna Singer

Editors: Risa Cottler, Susan Garver, Amy Lewis, Linda Scher, Betty Shanley, Bonnie Swaim, Frances Wiser

Production Supervisor: Mary Lyn Sodano

Inputting: Cindy Feldner

Interior Design: Maxson Crandall

Cover Design: Mike McIver

Layout: Maxson Crandall, Lisa Evans, Graphic Typesetting Service, Elizabeth Onorato

Photo Research: Cynthia Cappa, Sara Matthews

Maps: Parrot Graphics

Graphs: Virtual Media

Proofreading Management: Amy Davis

Grateful acknowledgment is made for permission to reprint the following previously published material:

"First Fig" by Edna St. Vincent Millay. From *Collected Poems*, Harper & Row. Copyright 1922, 1950, by Edna St. Vincent Millay. Reprinted by permission of Elizabeth Barnet, literary executor.

"Happy Days Are Here Again" by Milton Ager and Jack Yellen. Copyright 1929 by Warner Bros. Inc. (Renewed) All rights reserved. Used by permission.

Photo Credits

American Heritage Picture Collection: 3 (5th from left), 86

AP/Wide World Photos: 3 (far right), 104

Authenticated News International: 101

Bettmann/Hulton: 55, 81

Brown Brothers: 109

Coca-Cola Co.: 28

Culver Pictures, Inc.: 3 (2nd; 3rd from left), 15, 33, 34, 42, 49 (top), 58, 68 (bottom), 78 (top), 116 (right)

From the Collections of the Henry Ford Museum and Greenfield Village: 3 (4th from left), 74

Motor Vehicle Association: 68 (top)

National Museum of American Art, Washington, DC/Art Resource, NY: 102

Photoworld/FPG International: 54

Springer/Bettmann Film Archive: 98 (left)

The Bettmann Archive: 3 (far left), 10, 14, 17, 19, 25, 29, 31, 41, 45, 49 (bottom), 57, 61, 67, 73, 78 (bottom), 82, 85, 88, 91, 92 (both), 96, 97 (both), 98 (right), 99, 100, 103, 106, 107, 113, 116 (left)

The Granger Collection: 36, 40, 44, 47, 65, 79, 95

The Library of Congress: 62

UPI/Bettmann: 12, 18, 21, 30, 48, 51, 60, 69, 76, 80 (both), 90, 108, 111, 112, 114, 115, 117 (left)

UPI/Bettmann Newsphotos: 23, 27, 64, 117 (right)

Wide World Photos: 37

Macmillan Publishing Company
866 Third Avenue
New York, NY 10022

Maxwell Macmillan Canada, Inc.
1200 Eglinton Avenue East, Suite 200
Don Mills, Ontario M3C 3N1

Macmillan Publishing Company is part of the Maxwell Communication Group of Companies

Printed in the United States of America

printing number
1   2   3   4   5   6   7   8   9   10

Library of Congress Cataloging-in-Publication Data

The twentieth century / consultants, Matthew T. Downey . . . [et al.].
    p.   cm.
    Includes index.
    Contents: v. 1. The Progressive Era and the First World War (1900–1918)—v. 2. The Roaring Twenties and an Unsettled Peace (1919–1929)—v. 3. The Great Depression and World War II (1930–1945)—v. 4. Postwar Prosperity and the Cold War (1946–1963)—v. 5. The Civil Rights Movement and the Vietnam Era (1964–1975)—v. 6. Baby Boomers and the New Conservatism (1976–1991).
    ISBN 0-02-897442-5 (set : alk. paper)
    1. History, Modern—20th century. I. Downey, Matthew T.
D421.T88 1992
909.82—dc20
                            91-40862

Preface

The Twentieth Century is a six-book series covering the major developments of the period, from a primarily American perspective. This is the chronicle of a century unlike any before, one in which the pace of change has accelerated to the point that it is almost overwhelming.

As the century draws to a close, with such major ongoing events as the end of the Cold War and the seeming collapse of communism, it is appropriate to step back from the furious rush forward and examine the significance of the many changes we have seen in what may be the most momentous epoch in the history of the world.

Here, then, is the story of a world transformed by technology: by radio, television, and satellite communications; by automobiles, airplanes, and space travel; by antibiotics, organ transplants, and genetic engineering; by the atomic bomb; by the computer. These are just a few of the advances that have revolutionized the workings of the world and our daily lives.

Here also is the story of a century of history strongly influenced by individuals: Vladimir Lenin and Mao Ze-dong; Franklin Delano Roosevelt, Winston Churchill, and Adolf Hitler; Lech Walesa and Mikhail Gorbachev; Mohandas Gandhi and Martin Luther King Jr.; Theodore Roosevelt, John F. Kennedy, and Ronald Reagan. All have been featured actors in the drama of our times, as conveyed by these pages.

Above all else, it is the story of an American century, one in which a young democratic nation emerged as the world's most powerful force. Through two bitter world wars and an enduring cold war, the dominant influence of the United States on twentieth-century world history and culture is undeniable.

It is the story of the many forces that have transformed the face of our nation from a primarily rural, agricultural society dominated by white people of European heritage to a modern urban, industrialized, and multicultural nation. It is a story of the challenges, successes, and failures that have accompanied these fundamental changes.

Each book of this series focuses on a distinct era of the century. The six titles in the series are:

*The Progressive Era and
the First World War (1900–1918)*

*The Roaring Twenties and
an Unsettled Peace (1919–1929)*

*The Great Depression
and World War II (1930–1945)*

*Postwar Prosperity
and the Cold War (1946–1963)*

*The Civil Rights Movement
and the Vietnam Era (1964–1975)*

*Baby Boomers and the
New Conservatism (1976–1991)*

Each book is divided into six units: The Nation, The World, Business and Economy, Science and Technology, Arts and Entertainment, and Sports and Leisure. The second page of each unit includes a Datafile presenting significant statistical information in both table and graph format. All units include boxed features and sidebars focusing on particular topics of interest.

Additional features of each book include a graphic timeline of events of the period called Glimpses of the Era; a compilation of quotes, headlines, slogans, and literary extracts called Voices of the Era; a glossary of terms; a list of suggested readings; and a complete index.

The series is illustrated with historical photos, as well as original maps, graphs, and tables conveying pertinent statistical data.

Contents

AT A GLANCE

Preface **5**

Glimpses of the Era **8**

The Nation **10**

The World **34**

Business and Economy **58**

Science and Technology **74**

Arts and Entertainment **86**

Sports and Leisure **104**

Voices of the Era **118**

Glossary **122**

Selected Readings **124**

Index **125**

The Nation 10

PEACE AND POLITICS **11**
The Paris Peace Conference **11**
The League of Nations **12**

REPUBLICAN LEADERSHIP **13**
Harding's "Normalcy" **13**   Coolidge's
"Stability" **15**   Hoover's "Prosperity" **16**

CHANGE AND PROSPERITY **17**
The Great Migration **17**   Urban
Expansion **19**   A Work Revolution **19**
Problems for a Consumer Society **21**

WOMEN AND THE BALLOT **22**
Pioneers for Women's Rights **22**
The Nineteenth Amendment **23**
New Voting Patterns **24**

PROHIBITION **24**
The Temperance Movement **24**   The
Effects of Prohibition **26**   Bootlegging
and Crime **26**   The Folly of
Enforcement **28**

A TIME OF NATIONAL ANXIETY **29**
The Red Scare **30**   The Ku Klux
Klan **32**

Features: Harding Emerges from the
Smoke-Filled Room **14**   Marcus
Garvey (1887–1940) **18**   Legendary
Mobster Al Capone **27**   Coca-Cola
Prospers with Prohibition **28**
Immigration Quotas: Keeping America
"American" **32**

The World 34

AN OLD-STYLE PEACE **35**
The Fourteen Points **35**   The Paris
Peace Conference **36**   The Finished
Treaty **37**

A NEW WORLD ORDER **38**
The League of Nations **38**
U.S. Moves **39**

THE RISE OF THE USSR **40**
The Russian Revolutions **40**
"Red" Versus "White" **42**   The New
Economic Policy **42**   Socialism in
Russia **43**   Stalin's New Direction **43**

THE AFTERSHOCKS OF WAR IN EUROPE 44
The Money Problem **45**   New
Republics **46**   Great Britain **46**
France **46**   Italy **47**   Germany **48**

CHANGE IN THE MIDDLE EAST **49**
Too Many Promises **49**   Arab
Reaction **50**   A Legacy of Hate **53**

MOVES TOWARD INDEPENDENCE **53**
China **53**   India **54**   Africa **55**
Latin America's New Stance **56**

Features: The League of Nations
and the Tragedy of Armenia **39**
Revolution and Famine: Russia's Time
of Suffering **41**   Young Joseph Stalin:
The Making of a Dictator **44**   Eamon
De Valera and Irish Independence **47**
Kemal Atatürk: Father of Modern
Turkey **51**   Arab Nations Achieve
Self-Determination **52**

Business and Economy 58

ECONOMIC UPS AND DOWNS **59**
A Slow Start **59**   Economic
Expansion **60**   The Workforce **60**

KEYS TO PROSPERITY **62**
Corporate Growth **62**   Efficient
Management **63**   Increasing
Productivity **63**   Industrial Growth **63**
The Booming Stock Market **63**

A CONSUMER ERA **64**
Higher Incomes **64**   New Products **64**
Lower Prices **65**   Installment
Plans **65**   An Advertising Age **66**

THE AUTOMOTIVE AGE **67**
An Industrial Explosion **68**   A Social
Revolution **69**

SIGNS OF WEAKNESS   70
The Farming Crisis **71**   The Stormy
Stock Market **72**   The Crash **73**

Features: Black Labor Organizer
A. Philip Randolph **61**   The Mass
Retailing Revolution **67**   Alfred P.
Sloan: A New Kind of Automaker **69**

Science and Technology 74

TIME-SAVING TECHNIQUES   75
The Moving Assembly Line **75**
Household Appliances **76**

THE AIRPLANE INDUSTRY TAKES OFF   77
Barnstorming **77**   Flying the Mail **77**
Coast to Coast **77**   Aviation Firsts **78**

THE BROADCASTING BOOM   79
Radio Comes of Age **79**   Early
Programs **80**   Radio Networks **81**

**THE DISCOVERY OF INSULIN
AND PENICILLIN**   81
A Matter of Luck **82**

THE MYSTERY OF MATTER   83

THE SCOPES TRIAL   84

Features: The Uncertainty Concerning
Uncertainty **83**   The New Galaxies of
Astronomer Edwin Hubble **84**

Arts and Entertainment 86

THE JAZZ AGE   87
Jazz's Development **87**   King Oliver **88**
The Spread of Jazz **89**   George
Gershwin **89**

THE HARLEM RENAISSANCE   89
A New Spirit **90**   Continuing the
Challenge **90**

THE WRITER'S ART   91
Cynical Novels **92**   Stimulating
Poetry **93**   The Popular Press **94**

A LIVELY ERA ON STAGE   95
Mass Entertainment **95**   Serious
Drama **96**   The Birth of Modern
Dance **96**

THE MOVIES LEARN TO SPEAK   98
Screen Idols **98**   New Movie
Trends **100**

**ENTERTAINMENT ENTERS
AMERICA'S LIVING ROOMS**   101

**NEW STYLES IN ART AND
ARCHITECTURE**   102
Varied Art **102**   Form and
Function **103**

Features: Jazz Trumpeter Louis
"Satchmo" Armstrong **88**   Langston
Hughes: Voice of Harlem **91**
American Literature and the Lost
Generation **93**   Homespun Humorist
Will Rogers **95**   Religion as Theater:
Evangelists Sunday and McPherson **97**
Film Stardom and the Transition to
Sound **99**

Sports and Leisure 104

**THE GOLDEN AGE
OF SPORTSWRITING**   105

SPORTS' GROWING INFLUENCE   106
Fads, Games, and Leisure
Pursuits **106**

**BASEBALL COMES BACK
FROM THE BRINK**   107
A Game at Risk **107**   A New
Image **108**   The Sultan of Swat **108**
The Georgia Peach **109**   The Negro
and Minor Leagues **110**

**COLLEGE FOOTBALL'S
GREATEST LEGENDS**   110
Knute Rockne **110**   Red Grange **111**
The Professional Game **111**

THE DEMPSEY-TUNNEY ERA   111
Jack Dempsey **112**   Gene
Tunney **112**   The Match of the
Decade **112**

**TILDEN AND WILLS
MAKE TENNIS BIG**   113
Master Showman **113**   No-Nonsense
Tennis **114**

THE LEGENDARY BOBBY JONES   114
Bobby Jones **115**   Other Golfing
Greats **115**

**THE CHAMPION AND
THE CHANNEL SWIMMER**   117

Features: Horse Racing's Brightest Star:
Man o' War **109**   Jones and Ruth:
Sporting Styles of the Decade **116**

Jan. 5   Adolf Hitler joins discussion group; renames it Nazi party in 1920

Jan. 6   Theodore Roosevelt dies

Jan. 25   Paris Peace Conference adopts principle of League of Nations

Feb. 23   Benito Mussolini founds Fascist party in Italy

Mar. 15   American Legion organized

June 2   Poet Carl Sandburg wins Pulitzer Prize for *Cornhuskers*

June 29   Sir Barton becomes first horse to win Triple Crown

Aug. 11   Andrew Carnegie dies

▶ 1919

Mar. 4   Warren G. Harding becomes 29th president

May 31   Race riots in Tulsa, Oklahoma, leave 79 dead

June 30   President Harding names former president William H. Taft chief justice of the U.S. Supreme Court

July 29   Adolf Hitler becomes president of Nazi party

Sept. 7   First Miss America pageant held

Nov. 5   President Harding declares Armistice Day a legal holiday

▶ 1921

Jan. 1   Evangelist Aimee Semple McPherson opens $1.5 million Angelus Temple

Jan. 10   U.S. withdraws last troops from Germany

Jan. 18   British Broadcasting Company receives license

Feb. 12   *Rhapsody in Blue* by George Gershwin premieres

Feb. 16   Singer Bessie Smith makes her first recording, "Downhearted Blues"

Sept. 1   Earthquake in Tokyo kills more than 100,000 and leaves millions homeless

Nov. 6   Jacob Schick patents first electric razor

Dec. 25   White House erects its first electrically lit Christmas tree

▶ 1923

Jan. 5   Radio Corporation of America (RCA) founded

Jan. 10   Treaty of Versailles goes into effect

Jan. 16   Prohibition begins in U.S.

Aug. 1   Universal Negro Improvement Association, led by Marcus Garvey, begins monthlong convention in Harlem, New York City

Aug. 26   19th Amendment ratified, giving women the vote

Nov. 2   Pittsburgh station KDKA begins first national radio broadcasts

1920 ◀

Feb. 5   First issue of *Reader's Digest* published in U.S.

Apr. 16   The Senate begins investigating Teapot Dome scandal

Apr. 21   Lee De Forest invents device that records voice and image on the same film

Aug. 1   Telephone inventor Alexander Graham Bell dies

Oct. 3   Rebecca Felton becomes first woman senator

Oct. 31   Benito Mussolini becomes prime minister of Italy

1922 ◀

Jan. 21   Vladimir Lenin dies

Feb. 3   Woodrow Wilson dies

Feb. 14   The Computing-Tabulating-Recording Company renamed International Business Machines

June 2   U.S. grants full citizenship to Native Americans

Aug. 5   *Little Orphan Annie* comic strip, created by cartoonist Harold Gray, debuts in *New York Daily News*

Oct. 8   National Lutheran Conference bans use of jazz in churches

1924 ◀

GLIMPSES OF THE ERA

Jan. 5   Nellie Tayloe Ross becomes first woman governor

Mar. 4   Calvin Coolidge is first president to have inauguration broadcast over radio

July 10   John T. Scopes goes on trial for teaching theory of evolution in Tennessee

Nov. 28   First country music program, *Barn Dance*, aired on radio station WSM in Nashville, Tennessee

▶ 1925

Feb. 18   U.S. opens diplomatic relations with Canada, independent of Britain

May 16   Supreme Court rules that "bootleggers" must file income tax returns

May 20   Charles Lindbergh begins first nonstop solo flight across Atlantic Ocean

July 29   Dr. Philip Drinker and Dr. Louis A. Shaw operate "iron lung" at Bellevue Hospital in New York City

Sept. 22   Gene Tunney defends heavyweight boxing title against Jack Dempsey

Sept. 26   William S. Paley founds Columbia Broadcasting System (CBS)

Sept. 30   Babe Ruth hits 60th home run of the season, a new record

Dec. 4   Duke Ellington's band opens at Harlem's Cotton Club

▶ 1927

Feb. 14   Six gangsters killed by rivals in St. Valentine's Day Massacre

Apr. 15   Birth Control Clinical Research Center, established in New York City by Margaret Sanger, raided by New York police

May 16   First Academy Awards presented at banquet in Hollywood

July 1   Cartoon character Popeye created by Elzie Segar

Oct. 24   Black Tuesday

Nov. 8   Museum of Modern Art opens in New York City

▶ 1929

Mar. 16   Massachusetts physicist Robert H. Goddard launches first liquid-fuel rocket

Apr. 17   Mauna Loa volcano in Hawaii erupts

Apr. 26   Mae West arrested for performing belly dance in the play *Sex*

May 5   Sinclair Lewis refuses Pulitzer Prize for *Arrowsmith*

Aug. 6   Gertrude Ederle is first woman to swim English Channel

Aug. 23   Film star Rudolph Valentino dies

Sept. 25   Automaker Henry Ford institutes 40-hour, 5-day workweek at his company

Oct. 6   Babe Ruth hits 3 home runs in fourth game of World Series, a new record

Oct. 31   Magician Harry Houdini dies

Nov. 11   Route 66, from Chicago to Los Angeles, opens

Dec. 25   Hirohito becomes Japanese emperor

1926 ◀

Jan. 3   U.S. sends troops to Nicaragua to fight rebels

Mar. 12   St. Francis Dam in California bursts, causing major flooding and many deaths

Apr. 3   Lewis Carroll's original *Alice in Wonderland* manuscript purchased in U.S. for $75,260

Apr. 23   Actress/diplomat Shirley Temple born

May 28   Chrysler and Dodge Motors merge

June 17   Amelia Earhart sets out from Boston on flight across Atlantic, becoming first woman to do so

Oct. 6   Jiang Jie-shi (Chiang Kai-shek) becomes head of Nationalist party in China

Nov. 6   First animated electric sign in U.S. mounted around Times Building by *New York Times*

Nov. 18   Mickey Mouse debuts in *Steamboat Willie*

1928 ◀

THE NATION

The year was 1919, World War I was over, and Americans were in a mood to forget it. While President Woodrow Wilson was working earnestly at the Paris Peace Conference, many Americans were interested in getting on with their lives. Rejecting the Versailles treaty and the League of Nations, voters elected three Republican presidents during the 1920s. These presidents believed that the business of the nation was business. Under their leadership the nation's economy prospered, if unevenly, and its cities, such as New York (above), grew spectacularly.

American factories, which had worked overtime to mass-produce goods for the war effort, now applied their technology to making cars, radios, washing machines, refrigerators, and other consumer goods. As business increased, jobs be-

AT A GLANCE

- ▶ **Peace and Politics**
- ▶ **Republican Leadership**
- ▶ **Change and Prosperity**
- ▶ **Women and the Ballot**
- ▶ **Prohibition**
- ▶ **A Time of National Anxiety**

came plentiful. With money to spend, people found plenty to buy.

Along with prosperity, however, the 1920s brought change and conflict. With the ratification of the Nineteenth Amendment, women began to exert their political influence in the voting booth and in elected office. The Eighteenth Amendment and the Volstead Act made the manufacture and sale of liquor illegal, but many Americans drank anyway, supplied with liquor imported illegally or produced domestically in stills and breweries owned and operated by organized crime. Many people became more materialistic in their wants and needs and less conservative in their thinking. For others, however, the changes taking place were threatening, and they looked for ways to preserve what was familiar to them.

U.S. population	1920	1930
Total (in millions)	105.7	122.8
Urban	51.2%	56.2%
Rural	48.8%	43.8%
White	89.7%	89.8%
Black	9.9%	9.7%
Other	0.4%	0.5%

Social data	1919	1929
Birthrate (live births per 1,000 pop.)	26.1	21.2
Mortality rate (per 1,000 pop.)	12.9	11.9
Murder rate (per 100,000 pop.)	7.2	8.4

	1918	1928
Persons aged 5–17 in school (per 100 pop.)	81.8	89.1

Voter turnout	
1920	49.2%
1924	48.9%
1928	56.9%

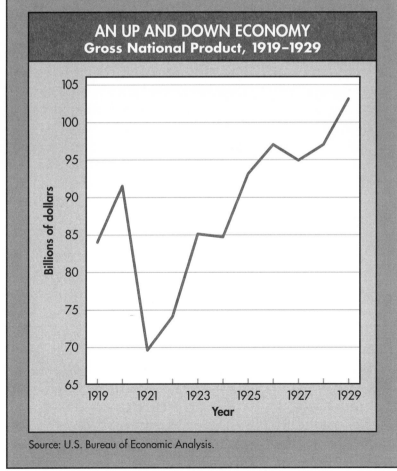

AN UP AND DOWN ECONOMY
Gross National Product, 1919–1929

Source: U.S. Bureau of Economic Analysis.

PEACE AND POLITICS

America's industrial might had helped save Europe from the tyranny of the Central Powers by its intervention in World War I. At the end of the war, many Europeans looked to Wilson's Fourteen Points as the basis of a just and lasting peace settlement. When the United States had entered the war, Americans had rallied behind Wilson's call to "make the world safe for democracy."

But the war was now over, and they were ready to move on. They tired of Wilson's idealism and rejected the Treaty of Versailles. They also rejected Wilson's efforts to build a system of **collective security** through the League of Nations. Instead, they turned their backs on Europe and retreated into a period of isolation that lasted throughout most of the 1920s.

The Paris Peace Conference

Midmorning on December 13, 1918, the huge shore guns at the French port city of Brest began to fire, shattering the peaceful air with their thunder. Far from a threat, the message of the guns was a welcome to Woodrow Wilson. When Wilson sailed into Brest that day, he became the first American president to visit a European nation while he was in office.

As Wilson entered Paris the next day, 36,000 French troops lined his route into the city. Hundreds of thousands of people cheered him, waving banners that read, "Hail to the Champion of the

President Woodrow Wilson addresses a crowd in San Diego during his League of Nations Peace Tour in September 1919. Just days later Wilson suffered a stroke after collapsing during a similar speech in Pueblo, Colorado. His exact condition was treated as a closely guarded secret by his wife Edith, seen here in white.

THE COST OF REPARATIONS

Germany's war reparations were set at $56 billion. Never before had a defeated warring nation been punished so severely.

Rights of Man" and "Welcome to the Founder of the Society of Nations." One journalist reported, "No one ever had such cheers. I, who heard them in the streets of Paris, can never forget them in my life." Throughout Europe the people cheered Wilson, believing his ideas held the brightest hope for their future peace and prosperity.

In January 1919, only the representatives of the 27 victorious Allied nations involved in the war met at the Palace of Versailles outside Paris to write a peace treaty. Each national leader had his own ideas about the peace settlement, especially those known as the "Big Four": France's Georges Clemenceau, Great Britain's David Lloyd George, Italy's Vittorio Orlando, and Woodrow Wilson of the United States.

Wilson was the idealist; he wanted the peace treaty to be based on "the eternal principles of right and justice." He believed each nation in Europe should be free to decide its own destiny, within boundaries that followed "clearly recognizable lines of nationality."

Other Allied leaders had different ideas. They wanted **reparations,** compensation for war damages. They also wanted Germany and the other Central Powers to be punished. "Mr. Wilson bores me with his fourteen points," said Clemenceau. "Even God Almighty has only ten!" Clemenceau proposed that Germany be divided and disarmed. Orlando wanted territories held by the Austro-Hungarian Empire that had been promised to Italy in a secret treaty signed in 1915. The leaders of Great Britain and Japan wanted German possessions in Africa and the Pacific.

During months of negotiating, Wilson was forced to give way on almost all of his Fourteen Points. Signed on June 28, the Treaty of Versailles forced Germany to admit guilt for the war, give up territory, disarm, and pay heavy reparations. But the treaty also provided for Wilson's League of Nations. One by one Wilson compromised on his other 13 points to save the League, believing it could keep the peace and soften the harsh requirements of the treaty.

The League of Nations

While Wilson was busy making peace in Paris, Americans at home were concerned about their jobs and what would happen to the economy. When Wilson returned from Paris, he found that the country cared little about his treasured League of Nations.

Wilson also found the Senate in an ugly mood. Many senators, including Henry Cabot Lodge of

Massachusetts, were angered that Wilson had failed to invite them to Paris or to involve them in earlier decisions about the peace settlement. Sensing the Senate's mood, Wilson took his case directly to the people, traveling through the Midwest and the West to speak in favor of the League. Wilson's physical strength, however, was no match for his heavy schedule. He collapsed on September 25, 1919, following a speech in Pueblo, Colorado, and suffered a stroke several days later.

While Wilson slowly regained his strength, he stubbornly refused to work with Lodge and the Republicans on a compromise version of the treaty. As a result, the Senate rejected the treaty in November 1919 and again in March 1920. In the 1920 presidential campaign, Wilson urged voters to elect his party's nominee, Democrat James M. Cox of Ohio. Cox supported the League. Warren Harding, the Republican nominee, took no firm stand on the issue.

Harding's overwhelming victory signaled the American voters' final rejection of Wilson's attempts to solve the international problems left by the war. Unappreciated at home, Wilson's efforts were recognized abroad in 1919, when he was awarded the Nobel Peace Prize.

REPUBLICAN LEADERSHIP

The decade was half over when President Calvin Coolidge noted that "the chief business of the American people is business. They are profoundly concerned with producing, buying, selling, investing, and prospering in the world."

As the 1920s began, most Americans had grown tired of ideals and crusades, of reforms and self-sacrifice. They wanted to mind their own business. And so they did. Business ruled during this period, both on the main streets of America and in the White House. While many people enjoyed prosperity, many others found it an impossible dream. For most, the dream had turned into a nightmare by the end of the decade.

Harding's "Normalcy"

In 1920, the Republican party convention in Chicago deadlocked on a candidate to run against the Democratic ticket of James M. Cox and Franklin D. Roosevelt. Finally, party leaders turned to a compromise candidate, a newspaper publisher and U.S. senator from Ohio—Warren G. Harding. "This year we had a lot of second-raters," one Republican observed. "Harding is no world-beater. But he's the best of the second-raters."

Harding may not have impressed party leaders, but he knew exactly what the American people wanted and gave it to them in long, windy speeches he called "bloviating." "America's present need is not heroics, but healing," Harding proclaimed in a campaign speech. "Not nostrums, but normalcy; not revolution, but restoration; not agitation, but adjustment; not surgery, but serenity."

Many Americans liked the sound of his message, even if they were uncertain of his exact meaning. In the November election,

Harding beat the Democratic candidate by 7 million votes.

Harding was a handsome, good-humored man who pledged to appoint the "best minds" to his Cabinet. Accordingly, he appointed Charles Evans Hughes to be secretary of state, Andrew Mellon as secretary of the treasury, and Herbert Hoover as secretary of commerce, three men of outstanding ability.

Unfortunately, Harding also appointed Cabinet members of questionable character and ability.

The president seldom consulted any of them, however, relying for advice instead on a group of card-playing friends from Ohio called the "Poker Cabinet." At least five of Harding's poker buddies used their friendship with the president as a way to fill their pockets with taxpayers' money.

Perhaps the most-remembered symbol of Harding's presidency is the Teapot Dome scandal. Albert Fall, Harding's secretary of the interior, secretly leased government

Harding Emerges from the Smoke-Filled Room

In 1920, the Republican party had far too many men who wanted to be president. There were a general, a governor, one or two Cabinet members, and two senators—one of whom was Warren G. Harding.

Harry Daugherty, Harding's friend, knew about the problem and predicted what would happen. He said that the convention would vote again and again without selecting a candidate. It would be about two o'clock in the morning on the third day of the convention. Ten or 20 tired men— the ones who really had the power in the party—would be sitting in a room in the Blackstone Hotel in Chicago. Their eyes would be red from all the smoke in the room.

After two days of arguing over the candidates, they would be ready for a

new idea. Daugherty would present that idea, and it would be in the form of Ohio senator Warren G. Harding. Harding, Daugherty said, would become the Republican candidate for president.

▲ A Harding-Coolidge campaign button

That was almost exactly what happened. The "king-makers," as the men in the now-famous "smoke-filled room" were called, wanted someone who would follow their orders. They discussed whether Harding met this requirement. Before long, they called Harding into the room. They wanted to know whether he had done anything in the past that could embarrass the party. Harding thought for a few minutes, then told them that his conscience was clear.

The next day Harding was nominated as the Republican candidate for president. "We're in the Big League now," a delighted Harding told one of his good friends. Unfortunately, his clear record would become dirtied by the unethical acts of some of these same good friends.

oil fields that had been set aside for use by the Navy—including one at Teapot Dome, Wyoming—to wealthy friends. After a lengthy government investigation, Fall became the first Cabinet officer in history to go to prison for accepting bribes. The oil leases were later canceled.

Coolidge's "Stability"

When President Harding died in San Francisco on August 2, 1923, the news was flashed by telegraph to Vermont, where Vice President Calvin Coolidge was visiting his father. There an alert telegrapher realized the importance of the message and rode 12 miles through the night to deliver the message to Coolidge. At 2:47 A.M., by the light of a kerosene lamp, Coolidge's father, a notary public, administered the oath of office to his son.

In many ways, Coolidge and Harding were a study in contrasts. Unlike Harding, with his fondness for playing cards with his pals, Coolidge symbolized restraint and the old-fashioned virtues of his native New England. Rather than "bloviating" like Harding, Coolidge used words sparingly, so much so that he earned the nickname Silent Cal. Yet Coolidge's dry wit occasionally shone through his nononsense personality. When a dinner guest once approached the president to say, "Mr. Coolidge, I've made a rather sizable bet with my friends that I can get you to say three words this evening," the president replied, "You lose."

Coolidge's character may have differed from Harding's. But like his predecessor's, Coolidge's poli-

Who Says a Watched Pot Never Boils?

▲ The Teapot Dome scandal of the Harding administration inspired many editorial cartoons similar to the one above.

cies emphasized the Republican philosophy of rugged individualism. In response to an appeal for aid from flood victims in Mississippi, Coolidge replied, "The government is not an insurer of its citizens against the hazards of the elements." Coolidge had an equally hands-off approach to foreign policy.

Like Harding, Coolidge also had a commitment to big business. "This is a business country; it wants a business government," Coolidge once explained. Both

Warren Harding was the first president heard on the radio. The occasion was a speech delivered on June 12, 1922.

On December 6, 1923, Calvin Coolidge delivered an address to Congress. This was the first such address to be broadcast over the radio and was carried by several stations from Rhode Island to Texas. The broadcast was so clear that radio technicians in Missouri could hear the president turning the pages of his address.

"If you see ten troubles coming down the road, you can be sure that nine will run into the ditch before they reach you."

—Calvin Coolidge

PARKER ON COOLIDGE

Dorothy Parker, a poet and short-story writer popular during the 1920s, was known for her humor and cynical attitude. A perfect example was her response to being told that President Coolidge, known for his reserve, had died: "How could they tell?"

Harding and Coolidge believed that leaving big business alone was the best way to create prosperity. They supported big business through key appointments to the Supreme Court, regulatory agencies, and the Cabinet. The people appointed to government agencies that regulated big business were, as expected, business people who opposed regulation. As the decade progressed, big business became increasingly free to make its own rules.

Like Harding, Coolidge also appointed wealthy business people to his Cabinet. Andrew Mellon, for example, who served as secretary of the treasury under all three of the decade's presidents, was the third wealthiest person in the country. As secretary, Mellon successfully reversed many of the Progressive tax reforms of the Wilson years. By 1926, American millionaires paid less than one-third of the taxes they had paid in 1921.

Coolidge decided not to run for reelection in 1928. He offered no reason for his decision. As humorist Will Rogers put it, the president retired from office a hero "not only because he hadn't done anything, but because he had done it better than anyone else."

Hoover's "Prosperity"

Herbert Hoover's campaign slogans in 1928 gave the American people all the reasons they needed to elect him president over Al Smith, the Democratic candidate. "Help Hoover Help Business," one proclaimed; "Let's Keep What We've Got: Prosperity Didn't Just Happen," declared another. The twin

sources of prosperity, according to Hoover, were free enterprise and rugged individualism.

Even before he became president, Hoover was well known throughout the country. He had left his career as a mining engineer to manage the U.S. Food Administration during World War I. After the war, Hoover had directed efforts to feed starving war refugees in Europe. He had won high praise for his dedication and brilliant management in both positions.

Hoover had served both Harding and Coolidge as secretary of commerce. In that role, he had supported better nutrition for children and eight-hour workdays. His emphasis on conservation of natural resources had led to the Pollution Act of 1924, the first attempt to control coastline oil pollution. Hoover also had set up government agencies to regulate the growing airline and radio industries. He had done so many things so well that Coolidge called him the "Wonder Boy," and others gave him the title "Secretary for Domestic Affairs."

Although President Hoover worked hard to improve people's lives, he also dedicated his administration to promoting business interests. Even after the economy showed signs of serious weakness and the stock market collapsed in 1929, Hoover insisted: "The fundamental business of the country . . . is on a sound and prosperous basis." Later events proved that his optimism was misplaced, and by the time he took action, the nation was in the middle of a depression so severe that it would not be eased until World War II.

CHANGE AND PROSPERITY

For many people in the 1920s, life was better than it had ever been. In America's cities skyscrapers were towering upward as if to prove that the nation's future economic growth was unlimited. New suburbs were reaching outward as if to include everyone in the prosperity that industry was creating. But in the economic boom of the 1920s, many changes occurred that dramatically affected American society and culture.

The Great Migration

During the 1920s, many Americans were on the move, searching for their share of the prosperity that was sweeping the land. Because jobs were plentiful in the cities, especially in the northern half of the United States, many people migrated from rural areas to the cities, and from the South to the North. Between 1921 and 1930, more than 20 million Americans moved to cities. This growth changed forever the face of the nation's urban areas.

The northward migration of black Americans from the South had an especially dramatic impact on the nation's cities. A black worker in the South made 50 to 75 cents a day. In a northern factory, the same worker made $1.50 a day or even more. Lured by such opportunity, southern blacks left their homes in search of jobs in meat-packing plants in Chicago, on automobile assembly lines in Detroit, and in steel foundries in Pittsburgh.

For Blacks: Progress and Frustration

Black workers made great gains during the 1920s. Many moved from the farms of the South to the cities of the North. There they found jobs in factories like the one above. They helped make automobiles, appliances, steel, and other products for wages far in excess of any they had earned before.

While they made progress, black Americans continued to have far less opportunity than whites of similar background. They had a harder time finding jobs and were often paid less than whites for the same work. They faced similar discrimination in nearly every aspect of their daily lives, especially in housing.

After World War I, their frustration occasionally boiled over into confrontations with whites. Many American cities experienced significant race riots during this period.

TIME OF TENSION
Major Race Riots, 1919–1921

Omaha 1919
Chicago 1919
Washington, D.C. 1919
Tulsa 1921
Knoxville 1919
Elaine 1919
Longview 1919

In 1916, for example, only 50 black workers were employed by the Ford Motor Company. By 1926, black employees numbered 10,000. Drawn by the North's many industries, the black population of northern cities swelled. In Detroit it jumped from 40,000 in 1920 to 120,000 in 1930. Over the same period, the black population in New York, Chicago, and Cleveland more than doubled.

Not everyone welcomed the increase in the number of black city dwellers. Competition for jobs and housing led to tensions between blacks and whites. At times, the racial tensions exploded into violence. During the hot summer of 1919, an ugly confrontation between blacks and whites erupted in Washington, D.C. It was fed by newspaper stories reporting rumors of an assault on a white

Marcus Garvey and the "Back to Africa" Movement

From the very beginning, Marcus Garvey was a man with a mission. Growing up in a large family in Jamaica, he was a black man in a white man's country. As a printer's apprentice in Kingston, Garvey learned about the poor conditions under which many blacks lived. He also learned that blacks needed to find a way to control their own destinies.

A journalist and admirer of Booker T. Washington, Garvey established the Universal Negro Improvement Association (UNIA) in 1914 while he was still in Jamaica. In 1916, he moved to New York, where he opened another branch of the UNIA and founded a black newspaper, the *Negro World.* Through the association and paper, he gained supporters for his "Back to Africa" movement.

Garvey thought that the only way blacks could gain control of their destinies was to return to Africa and establish their own country and government. He worked to foster world unity among blacks and to instill in blacks everywhere pride in the greatness of their heritage. A quarter of a million black people joined the UNIA, the largest grass-roots African-American movement until that time. UNIA had more than 30 branches at the height of its popularity.

Garvey was a master showman and a captivating speaker. He dressed in a fancy purple, black, and green uniform, and wore a hat with tall plumes. "Where is the black man's government?" Garvey would ask. "Where is his president, his country and ambassador, his army, his navy, his men of big affairs?" Then he would sound the theme of his "Back to Africa" movement: "Up, you mighty race."

Garvey founded the Black Star Line, an international shipping company that was to provide transportation and encourage trade among black businesses in New York, the West Indies, and Africa. Investors contributed about $500,000 to its establishment. When the line failed, Garvey was arrested and convicted of stock fraud in 1923. After a little more than two years in prison, he was deported to Jamaica, where his influence decreased.

woman by one or more blacks. In response, the chief of police ordered all blacks found on the streets after dark to be questioned and searched. Following this order, 200 white servicemen marched into the city and began to beat black residents. A group of blacks fought back, some using guns against whites who drove or walked through their neighborhood. The riot raged for four days. Finally, federal troops were called in to restore calm. The riot, however, left four people dead and dozens injured. Similar scenes of racial violence were repeated in many cities during the early 1920s.

Urban Expansion

America's cities expanded in two directions during the 1920s: upward and outward. Skyscrapers became towering symbols of the upward expansion and the nation's vast size, as well as the power of its economy and the vision of its people. One European visitor to New York described the tall buildings as "the dwellings of the super-companies. They are cathedrals which shelter Mr. Rockefeller, the Emperor of Petroleum, or Mr. Morgan, the Czar of Gold." The Tribune Tower in Chicago, the Petroleum Building in Houston, the Bank of Manhattan and the Chrysler Building in New York City, and the Terminal Tower in Cleveland all were completed by the end of the decade.

Cities expanded outward as well. Between 1920 and 1930, the residential suburb emerged as the community of the future. The mass production of automobiles allowed middle-class workers to live out-

▲ Workers lower the top of a massive stone column into position during construction of a building in St. Louis.

side city centers. The number of registered autos leaped from 9 million to 26 million—enough to put the entire population of the United States on the road at the same time.

A Work Revolution

The business boom of the 1920s led to yet another change in American culture: a revolution in labor. The expanding industrial economy needed new types of workers—

GROWING SKYSCRAPERS
By 1929 American cities had 377 skyscrapers more than 20 stories high.

managers, supervisors, sales personnel, and such office staff as bookkeepers, secretaries, typists, and file clerks. They became known as "white-collar" workers. Their number increased almost 40 percent during the decade; in contrast, the number of manual laborers, or "blue-collar" workers, increased by less than 10 percent over the same period. Many of the new white-collar jobs were provided by the auto industry, which quickly became the nation's largest. Fast-growing banks and insurance companies also added to the demand for white-collar workers.

The efficient, low-cost production of autos, vacuum cleaners, washing machines, and other goods was a new development. It fostered the growth of a consumer society, which was promoted by advertising. Ads blossomed everywhere—on billboards, in the newspapers, and over radio stations. "Drink Coca-Cola, the pause that refreshes," they suggested to a thirsty nation. "Wash with Palmolive for that schoolgirl complexion." Selling all types of consumer products became a thriving high-pressure business that fueled the demand for more consumer goods.

All the new white-collar workers helped make up a growing middle class in American society. People in the middle class earned their money in new ways, and they also spent it in new ways. Their incomes typically enabled them to afford an automobile and a house in the suburbs. Many could also afford to buy a wide range of home appliances and consumer products intended to make their lives easier and more enjoyable.

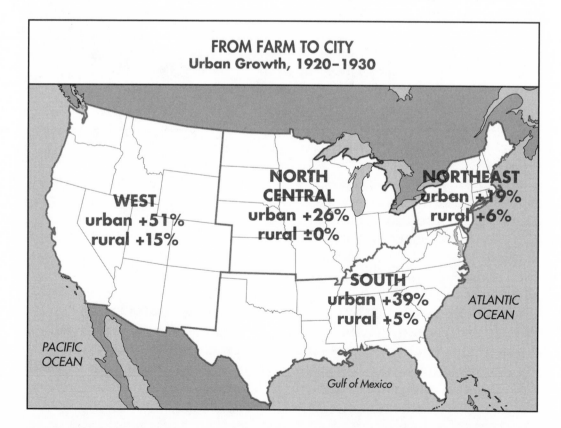

FROM FARM TO CITY
Urban Growth, 1920–1930

WEST
urban +51%
rural +15%

NORTH CENTRAL
urban +26%
rural ±0%

NORTHEAST
urban +19%
rural +6%

SOUTH
urban +39%
rural +5%

PACIFIC OCEAN

ATLANTIC OCEAN

Gulf of Mexico

▶ The population of America's cities grew much more quickly than that of its rural areas during the 1920s. This trend reflected the fact that most new jobs were created by urban businesses and factories.

◄ When the crash finally came, many Americans found their financial circumstances ruined overnight. Like this man, many were forced to sell their possessions in order to pay their bills.

Problems for a Consumer Society

In the 1920s business people became heroes and the pursuit of the almighty dollar took on the appearance of a crusade. Between 1922 and 1928, industrial production rose by 70 percent. With many jobs paying better, people had more money to spend. Or so it seemed. The real story was slightly less rosy and more complex. While many people and industries enjoyed overall prosperity, the nation's economy went through several major ups and downs.

By 1929, the wealthiest 5 percent of the population received about one-third of the nation's total personal income, leaving the other 95 percent to share the rest. Such an unequal distribution of wealth and purchasing power put a limit on the quantity of industrial products consumers could buy. It was this fundamental limitation that eventually undid the prosperity of the 1920s. When the demand for new goods was satisfied, the economy crashed.

One sector of the economy that was troubled throughout the decade was agriculture. Farmers became the victims of their own efficiency. Because America's farms produced surplus crops, crop prices remained low. In some cases, farmers received so little return on their harvests that they could not afford to plant new crops the next season. Farmers who were unable to make a living were forced to leave their farms to look for jobs in the cities.

Many other workers were poorly paid, and they had to struggle just to earn enough money to buy necessities. The black and white **sharecroppers** who remained in the South suffered most of all. Few earned more than $350 a year. Advances in technology also caused serious problems for some workers. For example, many textile workers in New England and coal miners in Pennsylvania and West Virginia lost their jobs to machines that were able to do the work faster and at a lower cost.

As a result, the combination of unemployment and low wages left one-third of all Americans living in poverty. These people knew nothing of silk stockings and white gloves, Niagara Blue roadsters and automatic washing machines. They never experienced the boom times of the 1920s.

WOMEN AND THE BALLOT

Early in the twentieth century, **Progressives** achieved many important reforms in their attempt to make life better for the American people. World War I interrupted their efforts, but the need for reform was not forgotten. With the end of the war came a renewed call for women's **suffrage.**

Pioneers for Women's Rights

When Elizabeth Cady Stanton married in 1840, she refused to promise to obey her new husband, a major break with tradition and a signal that times were changing. Eight years later, Stanton founded the first women's rights assembly in America. She called for more liberal divorce laws, less-restrictive clothing for women, coeducation, and the right of married women to control their own property.

Stanton's bold example inspired Susan B. Anthony, another key early activist. Together these two pioneers formed in 1869 what eventually became the National American Woman Suffrage Association (NAWSA), an organization that worked for women to have the right to vote. Anthony herself was arrested three years later for attempting to vote. In her defense, she claimed that the Fourteenth and Fifteenth amendments, which gave blacks the right to vote, applied equally to all citizens, male and female. Although her argument went unheeded, Anthony became the recognized leader of the women's suffrage movement.

In 1913 Alice Paul added a new dimension to the women's movement when she formed the National Woman's Party (NWP). Paul was a tough-minded reformer who had spent several years in England, attending school and working with militant suffragists. She quickly adapted their direct action tactics for use in America. For example, Paul and other members of the NWP set up picket lines at the White House and burned a likeness of President Wilson. When the pickets were arrested, they and other activists went on hunger strikes. In this way, the NWP focused national attention on the cause of women's rights.

After Carrie Chapman Catt succeeded Susan B. Anthony as head of NAWSA, she came to disagree with Paul's strategy of militant action. Instead, Catt and NAWSA worked to build a nationwide network of women who were involved in local politics.

The leaders of NAWSA also reminded the nation how women helped in the fight against the Central Powers. During World War I,

EQUALITY IN MARRIAGE

For years, following tradition, American brides pledged to "obey" their spouses. In 1922, U.S. Episcopalians voted to replace *obey* in the wedding vows with *cherish*. Later *man and wife* became *husband and wife*. Both of these changes served to recognize equality in marriage.

when almost 5 million men left home for military duty, women stepped in to run farms, manage stores, and fill crucial jobs in factories. Taking over roles traditionally reserved for men, women worked in factories, producing tanks, trucks, guns, and other war supplies. After the war ended, many women were forced to give up their jobs to returning soldiers. But women had shown that they were able to do the same work as men. The leaders of NAWSA pointed to these accomplishments as evidence that women were equal to men and deserved the right to vote.

The Nineteenth Amendment

A proposed amendment to the Constitution giving women the right to vote in national elections was introduced in Congress in 1878. For 40 years, Congress refused to pass the amendment. By 1919, however, the pressure to grant suffrage to women became too strong to resist. Fifteen states had already granted women equal voting rights with men, proving that the women's movement, led by the NWP and NAWSA, had become a powerful political force. President Wilson, a Progressive reformer, also urged Congress to pass the proposed suffrage amendment and send it to the states for ratification.

After Congress passed the Nineteenth Amendment in June 1919, 35 states passed the amendment almost immediately. The issue then came before the Tennessee legislature. If it passed, equal suffrage for women would become the law of the land.

On the day of the vote, the Tennessee suffragists lacked two votes to win. Then Harry Burn, the youngest member of the legislature, remembered a letter he had received from his mother, a strong suffragist. "I have been watching to see how you stood, but have noticed nothing yet," she wrote. "Don't forget to vote for ratification." Harry took his mother's advice, and when another member of the legislature followed Burn's example, the Nineteenth Amendment became part of the U.S. Constitution on August 26, 1920. American women had won the right to vote.

In the presidential election of 1920, however, only one out of every three eligible female voters cast ballots. Carrie Chapman Catt of NAWSA decided that many women simply did not know how to use their new right. These women, she suggested, were unaware that women voters could have a decisive influence on the nation's political system. To address this problem, Catt formed a new organization in 1920, the

▼ The women below are casting their ballots in the presidential election of 1920, the first in which all American women had the right to vote.

League of Women Voters, which remains active today. The league's purpose was to educate women about voting and to get them involved in politics.

Through the league, women voters began to make their presence known. While women had held elected positions in some states prior to the passage of the Nineteenth Amendment, none had been elected governor of a state prior to 1924. In that year Nellie Tayloe Ross of Wyoming was elected governor to replace her husband in that office after his sudden death. Ross insisted that gender had little to do with success or failure. "A woman will succeed or fail," she said, "just as a man will succeed or fail, and it is difficult to . . . imagine that there is any real difference in the manner in which men and women approach intellectual or practical problems."

Several weeks after Ross became governor of Wyoming, Miriam "Ma" Ferguson took office as the governor of Texas, replacing her husband, who had recently been impeached. The *Boston Transcript* noted that Ferguson would govern "a region much larger than France, and more than five times as large as England, with a population greater than that of Ireland, and resources far beyond those of the German Reich . . . a position as proud as that of many famous queens of the past."

New Voting Patterns

The Nineteenth Amendment had effects far beyond the election of a few women to prominent political offices. The tradition of government "by the people, for the people" now included many new voices. At first women voted much like men, except when they supported special causes. For example, in 1921 women united to support an act that provided money to hire public health nurses, hold conferences on health issues, and educate new mothers. While many Americans applauded and some resisted the emergence of women as part of national politics, all agreed that the Nineteenth Amendment had reshaped the political landscape.

PROHIBITION

In 1919, the Eighteenth Amendment was added to the U.S. Constitution. It banned the manufacture, distribution, and sale of alcoholic beverages. President Hoover called **Prohibition** "a great social and economic experiment, noble in motive." However noble, Prohibition did not decrease the public's thirst for such alcoholic beverages as whiskey, scotch, gin, beer, and wine. In fact, estimates suggest that alcohol consumption doubled between 1921 and 1929.

The Temperance Movement

Prohibition was the result of two things: a century-long temperance movement and a war. More than 100 years before Prohibition, concerned citizens began warning about the ill effects of alcohol use, particularly among immigrants, city dwellers, and industrial workers.

FUTURE FEMINISTS

▶ **Bella Abzug** was born in 1920. From 1971 to 1977 she served in the U.S. House of Representatives, where she was known for her support of the women's liberation movement. She also supported civil rights legislation for blacks and other minorities.

▶ **Shirley Chisholm** was born in 1924. She became the first black woman member of the U.S. House of Representatives (1969–1983). In 1972 she campaigned for, but did not win, the Democratic nomination for president.

▶ **Betty Friedan** was born in 1921. She is credited with starting the women's equal rights movement in the United States through her book *The Feminine Mystique*. The book outlined the pressures society put on women to be housewives rather than to have careers of their own. In 1966 she helped found the National Organization for Women.

But alcohol consumption—and abuse—was not just for the working class. Then as now, beer, wine, and hard liquor were consumed by men and women of all social, religious, and occupational groups. Most considered it their individual right to choose whether or not to drink alcoholic beverages.

Those who were against such consumption were also a varied group. They tended, however, to be religious (usually Protestant), "high-minded" people who felt that drinking liquor indicated weakness of character in an individual and led directly to a variety of ills in society as a whole. On both moral and practical grounds, they regarded drinking alcohol as something wrong, something that ought to be prohibited.

Their forces began to organize in the nineteenth century. In 1826, the American Temperance Society was founded to convince people to abstain from drinking alcoholic beverages. It was followed in 1874 by the Women's Christian Temperance Union, which began its crusade against alcohol and drug use "to improve public morals." The Anti-Saloon League was formed in 1893 and eventually became a powerful political force in securing passage of the Eighteenth Amendment. In the early twentieth century, the efforts of these groups found favor within the Progressive movement. Many Progressives supported Prohibition laws, believing that banning alcohol would contribute to their general efforts to create an improved society. As a consequence of their joint efforts, these various groups began to have some success passing Prohibition

laws at the local level. Between 1905 and 1917, the number of states with laws forbidding the sale of alcohol increased from 5 to 26. Nevertheless, the sale and consumption of beer, wine, and hard liquor remained widespread.

When World War I broke out, the Anti-Saloon League, appealing to patriotism, declared that Germany's mightiest ally in the United States was liquor. The league charged that beer makers were using enough barley each day to make 11 million loaves of bread for the troops. In addition, both beer and pretzels were associated with Germany. In contrast, the league stood for God, America, and a sober soldier charging toward victory.

The temperance movement and the wartime shortage of grain finally convinced Congress to take action. The Eighteenth Amendment was passed by Congress in 1917 and, after speedy ratification by the required number of states,

▲ The constitutional amendment banning the manufacture, distribution, and sale of alcoholic beverages was passed in 1919 after decades of effort by a collection of temperance organizations. Here, one such organization is enrolling new members in the effort to make the nation "dry."

THE FAILURE OF PROHIBITION
Money Spent on Alcohol, 1919–1929

Amount spent (in billions of dollars) vs. Year

Source: *Historical Statistics of the United States.*

▲ Despite Prohibition, Americans were soon spending as much money on alcohol as they had when its sale was legal.

went into effect at midnight on January 16, 1920. Congress then passed the National Prohibition Act, also called the "Volstead Act," to provide the means for enforcing the amendment.

The Effects of Prohibition

After Prohibition, America became a dry nation, at least in theory. From the beginning, popular opinion about Prohibition was divided. While it was overwhelmingly approved of by many Protestants, some were against it. Catholics, too, were divided, although many approved of drinking. On the whole, the leaders of big business accepted Prohibition, but they were against strong enforcement of

the law. Nonetheless, many Americans, it seemed, believed a nation without liquor would be a better place. The Anti-Saloon League summarized that belief in its slogan, "Now for an era of clear thinking and clean living." The evangelist Billy Sunday said good-bye to "John Barleycorn," the mythic maker of drink: "You were God's worst enemy. You were Hell's best friend. . . . The reign of tears is over."

Seldom in American history, however, was a law disobeyed with such openness and enthusiasm. After years of war and the sacrifices it called for, many people were ready for "creature comforts." The intensity of the temperance advocates was matched only by the inventiveness of the people who wanted to keep drinking. The illegal production, distribution, sale, and consumption of liquor became an obsession to many Americans. An entire illegal industry developed to meet the growing demand.

Bootlegging and Crime

Enforcing Prohibition proved extremely difficult. Liquor was easy to make, easy to transport, and even easier to sell. The equipment to build a small still and make liquor cost only $6 or $7, resulting in the building of many home stills. One folk song humorously described the situation:

> Mother makes brandy from cherries;
> Pop distills whiskey and gin;
> Sister sells wine from the grapes on our vine—
> God, how the money rolls in!

The money attracted all classes of people to **bootlegging,** the illegal production and distribution of liquor. A still producing more than 13,000 gallons of whiskey a day was even discovered on the Texas farm of Senator Morris Sheppard, the author of the Eighteenth Amendment. Ambitious racketeers set up large stills in out-of-the-way places. Others smuggled in whiskey from Canada and rum from the Caribbean islands to meet the public's growing demand.

With billions of dollars to be made, crime became big business. Al Capone, the king of the Chicago rackets, and other gangsters hired armies of still operators, drivers, and gunners. They bought out hundreds of breweries, brewed their own brands, and transported the beer in armored trucks. They ambushed rival gangs, stole their liquor, and killed their leaders. The violence associated with bootlegging was an effect the temperance movement never foresaw.

When Prohibition came, the old-time saloons went underground and became secret drinking clubs, called "speakeasies." By 1925, about 100,000 speakeasies existed in New York City alone. Some big-city speakeasies provided their customers with coded membership cards, plush and exotic settings,

Legendary Mobster Al Capone

Al Capone was a bootlegger who thought of himself as a businessman. He resented people who objected to his illegal line of work. People needed something to quench their thirst, and Capone sold it to them. "When I sell liquor, it's bootlegging," Capone complained. "When my patrons serve it on a silver tray on Lake Shore Drive, it's hospitality."

In six short years, Capone had risen from washing dishes in a New York nightclub to controlling a Chicago-based crime organization that in 1927 took in as much as $100 million. Capone rode in an armored limousine followed by three cars full of bodyguards to keep him safe from rivals who sought revenge. He had an army of 700 thugs who made and sold his liquor, ran his many speakeasies, and kept the city's politicians in line.

By the end of the decade, Capone controlled the entire bootlegging industry from Canada to Florida. He ruled his territory with a machine gun, and people who differed with Capone seldom troubled him for long.

At first, the public was captivated by stories of Capone and other gangsters. But after Capone's thugs machine-gunned rival Bugs Moran and five of his gang on Valentine's Day in 1929, people grew outraged over the violence and corruption of organized crime. Capone became a symbol of the things people feared most: violence, lawlessness, and mass murder.

In spite of his violent tactics, however, Capone's career in crime was ended, not by a machine-gun bullet, but by failure to pay his federal income taxes. In 1931, Capone went to prison for tax evasion, serving 11 years. He died in 1947 at the age of 48.

Coca-Cola Prospers with Prohibition

"It is an ill wind that blows nobody good," wrote *Time* magazine of Prohibition in 1925. Prohibition had ruined many breweries and distilleries, and even some short-haul railroads that mainly carried their products. On the other hand, *Time* continued, "It greatly stimulated some new enterprises—particularly those relating to human thirst and its legal satisfaction."

The *Time* article went on to describe the "epidemic of temperance-drink companies" that were trying to quench the thirst of a dry nation. The most popular of these nonalcoholic drinks was Coca-Cola, "the pause that refreshes." By mid-decade, 8 million Americans were pausing each day for a Coca-Cola.

Coca-Cola became popular because it was part of what has been called "the golden dawn of total advertising." "It had to be good to get where it is," claimed one of the company's advertising slogans. One magazine advertisement from the period showed a smiling typist at her desk, one hand on the typewriter, a bottle of Coca-Cola in the other. The ad read, "Each busy day tends down-hill from that top-of-the-morning feeling with which you begin. Don't whip yourself as the day begins to wear. Pause and refresh yourself with an ice-cold Coca-Cola, and be off to a fresh start."

◄ The makers of Coca-Cola seized the opportunity provided by Prohibition as a chance to change America's drinking habits.

nightly entertainment, and scotch at $25 a bottle. Most speakeasies stayed in business by paying off the police and by constructing elaborate alarm systems as a means of protection against raids by federal authorities.

The Folly of Enforcement

The 1,550 federal agents who were charged with enforcing Prohibition had an impossible task. These agents had to protect 18,700 miles of coastline and inland borders from smugglers. They had to be "watchdogs" for industries that used alcohol legally to make everything from shaving cream to diesel engines. They also had to track down thousands of illegal stills in the United States and try to keep millions of people from drinking alcoholic beverages. Even with more agents, enforcement was impossible. As one congressman said: "It would take 250,000 policemen to enforce Prohibition in New York City—and another 200,000 to police the police."

People found many clever ways to evade the agents. They carried liquor in hip flasks and even in garden hoses wrapped around their waists. They hid the stuff in false books and in hollow canes. Even though agents were seizing a million gallons of liquor and 7 million gallons of beer each year by the mid-1920s, the war against illegal liquor had been hopelessly lost even before it had begun.

The agents' lack of effectiveness prompted countless jokes and endless newspaper cartoons. So did the antics of the two most famous federal agents, "Izzy" Einstein and "Moe" Smith. Neither looked like

the romantic image of a detective (both were short and roly-poly), but both displayed cleverness and wit as they did their duty. The two became well known for their elaborate disguises, which they used to gain entrance to speakeasies. Once, for example, they put on gravediggers' overalls to bust a speakeasy near a graveyard. In spite of their best efforts and those of other agents, however, the bootleg liquor flowed and speakeasies multiplied.

Prohibition made life in America more violent, especially in the cities. Open rebellion against Prohibition became almost a fad, and people who usually obeyed the law began to break it. More important perhaps, Prohibition changed the way people in America thought about drinking. The consumption of alcoholic beverages by women and young people increased dramatically. Women had a new chance to show their equality with men, and young people could demonstrate their rejection of adult authority. Overall the "noble experiment," as Hoover had labeled it, yielded unexpected results, few of them noble.

A TIME OF NATIONAL ANXIETY

By the end of World War I, most Americans lived in cities. The growth of the nation's urban and industrial centers brought many changes to American society. Immigrants continued to journey to America in search of hope and opportunity. Labor unions continued their struggle to improve workers' lives. New social and political ideas

URBAN MIGRATION

In 1920 the U.S. Census Bureau reported a total population of 106,021,537. It also reported that the majority of Americans were now living in cities of 2,500 people or more. (Any town with a population less than 2,500 was considered rural.)

In 1917 J. Edgar Hoover was appointed special assistant to Attorney General A. Mitchell Palmer. Hoover helped organize the deportation raids in which thousands of suspected radicals were jailed without regard to their constitutional rights.

In 1921 Hoover was appointed assistant director of the agency that became the Federal Bureau of Investigation (FBI). Three years later, he became its full-time director, serving in that position for 48 years.

When Hoover became director, he strengthened the organization by hiring talented people and promoting them on the basis of their performance. He also established the world's largest fingerprint file and a crime laboratory.

After Hoover's death in 1972, however, his image was tarnished by the revelation that the FBI had engaged in illegal spying on U.S. citizens.

threatened the conservative ways of many Americans. They wanted things to stay the same, and the prospect of change made them anxious. At times, they lashed out, showing the dark undersides of the American dream in fits of intolerance and prejudice.

The Red Scare

One source of national anxiety was the threat of communism. Americans knew that the communists had taken over Russia in the Bolshevik Revolution in 1917. Rumors of "Red" revolts sweeping across Europe made Americans even more uneasy and fearful that communists would try to start a revolution in America. Alarmed citizens passed along unfounded rumors. One proclaimed that a Bolshevik ship had landed in America full of gold that would be used to corrupt the nation. Another claimed that

submarines had landed on the coast, carrying flu germs to spread in the nation's movie theaters. But some of the threats were real, including the 18 bombs that were disguised as department store parcels and mailed to prominent business and political leaders in 1919.

Other events fueled the spreading hysteria of intolerance. America's steel and coal workers went on strike in the fall of 1919. Mainly underpaid immigrants who worked long hours in miserable conditions, these workers wanted fair treatment from their employers. Many people ignored the facts and chose instead to see the strikers as radicals and foreign intruders fired up by Bolshevik organizers. These fearful Americans were ready to see "an anarchist behind every alien, a Red agitator behind every union organizer, and a Communist

► Steelworkers wave their strike notices in Chicago in 1919. During America's Red Scare following the Russian Revolution, many Americans viewed strikers such as these as communists who wanted to destroy democracy.

behind every labor protest," as one observer put it.

A. Mitchell Palmer, the attorney general of the United States, began an aggressive antiforeigner crusade, in part to help his chances of securing a presidential nomination. On June 2, 1919, when bombs exploded in 8 cities across the nation, including one at Palmer's home in Washington, D.C., he staged raids on unions in 12 cities, looking for Bolsheviks and other radicals. By December, he had rounded up 249 suspected radicals, whom he sent to Russia on the *Bunford,* a ship the press nicknamed the "Soviet Ark." The following month, Palmer's agents arrested more than 7,000 suspects and held them in jail without proof that any of them had committed a crime.

The attorney general also warned the nation that communists would unleash a wave of immorality, theft, and murder in the United States, as he claimed they had done in Russia. He organized the National Guard and the police to protect America against a revolution that he said 60,000 communists would stage during May 1920. For a time, Palmer had the nation convinced that the threat was genuine. During 1919, 14 states passed antistrike laws. To limit the number of foreigners who could enter the United States, Congress adopted the Emergency Quota Act of 1919. Fifteen states made teaching schoolchildren in any language but English illegal. When none of Palmer's predictions came true, the Red Scare subsided, but antiforeign sentiment continued.

In 1921, Nicola Sacco and Bartolomeo Vanzetti were arrested, convicted, and sentenced to death for the 1920 murder of two people during a robbery in Massachusetts. Sacco and Vanzetti had no criminal records, but they both were Italian immigrants and **anarchists** with radical political views. At their trial, little evidence was presented to show they were guilty of murder.

To many Americans it seemed they were convicted only because they were foreign-born radicals. Nevertheless, the two were executed in 1927. Their case aroused great controversy. Even today, some people claim they were unfairly tried. However, a ballistics test conducted in 1961 suggests that Sacco's gun might have fired the fatal bullet. The debate surrounding the long, drawn-out case slowly helped turn away the tide of public intolerance and prejudice. In addition, the troubles on the economic front pushed the Red Scare and the Sacco and Vanzetti case out of the headlines and the American consciousness.

▲ The Sacco and Vanzetti case created much controversy around the world. Here supporters of the Italian immigrants are demonstrating on their behalf in London, England. While the pair was eventually found guilty of murder and executed, many still contend they were innocent of the crime.

The Ku Klux Klan

Even more extreme reactions to postwar changes began in the South. After the Civil War, the Ku Klux Klan (KKK) was founded by southern whites to terrorize newly freed blacks. Klan members covered themselves with white sheets and peaked hoods. Meeting secretly at night, they used burning crosses to spread their violent message of hate and terror. Their methods included beating and **lynching** black people (and sometimes their white supporters) and burning their homes.

Eventually the Klan declined and then died. But in 1915 it was created anew by "Colonel" William J. Simmons, an unsuccessful Atlanta minister. Simmons named himself Emperor and led a crusade to defend "rural values and racial purity." He and his fellow Klansmen directed their hatred not only at blacks, but also at all foreign-born people, Jews, and Catholics, anyone they felt was not "pure American." The second Klan developed its own elaborate rituals and secret language to separate its members from the "impure elements" in American society.

Immigration Quotas: Keeping America "American"

"Give me your tired, your poor, your huddled masses yearning to breathe free," Emma Lazarus's poem on the Statue of Liberty declared to immigrants entering New York Harbor. After World War I, however, many Americans thought the message should be changed. They feared that the refugees escaping the horrors of war were turning America into something other than America.

Some critics of the new immigration suggested certain races were inferior and ought to be kept out. Other critics pointed out that Americans might lose jobs to immigrant workers. All had forgotten the values America represented in the first place.

In 1915 President Wilson vetoed a bill that would have forced immigrants to pass a literacy test. In 1917 such a law was passed over Wilson's veto. After Wilson left office, Congress pushed through the National Origins Acts of 1921 and 1924. In its later form, the law tried to maintain America's ethnic mixture as it was in 1890, so that America would stay "American."

▼ ▼ ▼

The values America had represented in the first place were forgotten.

The number of people admitted from a country each year was not to exceed 2 percent of the number of people in the United States from that country in 1890. The year 1890 was chosen because it worked against people from such countries as Italy and Poland in southern and eastern Europe.

People from Ireland, England, France, and Germany, on the other hand, had come to America in large numbers before 1890.

The act was amended again in 1927. The base year for determining quotas was changed to 1920, and the limit on total immigration was placed at 150,000 per year. More than half were designated to be British and German immigrants.

While Asian immigrants were entirely excluded, immigration from within the Western Hemisphere was not limited. As a result, Canadians, Mexicans, and Puerto Ricans soon became the largest groups of immigrants to the United States.

The KKK remained a small society until 1920, when Edward Y. Clarke, a marketing genius, began promoting the Klan in an attempt to gain new members. So successful was his advertising that not even newspaper reports of the Klan's beating a lawyer in South Carolina, branding a bellhop in Dallas, and tarring and feathering an Episcopal minister and drowning two other men in Florida slowed its growth. By 1923, an estimated 5 million Americans had joined the Klan, and reports were that 3,500 new members throughout the nation were joining each day. Hiram Wesley Evans, the Emperor and Imperial Wizard of the Klan, believed the KKK now represented "the great mass of Americans of the old pioneer stock."

No longer a fringe movement, the Klan became strong in Detroit, Pittsburgh, Indianapolis, and other northern cities to which many blacks and immigrants had recently migrated. The Klan attacked Mexican-Americans in Texas, Japanese-Americans in California, Italians, Poles, and other immigrants from southern Europe as well as Jews in New York, and French Canadians in New England. Their tactics against their victims became increasingly violent. In one year, the Klan in Oklahoma was responsible for at least 2,500 beatings.

In the early 1920s, the Klan became powerful enough to dominate the governments of seven states in the South, West, and Midwest. In 1925, however, the Grand Dragon of the Indiana Klan was sentenced to life in prison for kidnapping and brutally abusing a young woman. Many people who once had been attracted to the Klan's ideal of moral purity left because of the organization's increasing violence and corruption. People also grew tired of Klan warnings about terrible things that never happened. By the start of the Great Depression, Klan membership had dwindled to almost nothing.

BIRTHS . . .

John Glenn, astronaut and senator, 1921

George Bush, president, 1924

Jimmy Carter, president, 1924

Martin Luther King Jr., civil rights leader, 1929

Jacqueline Kennedy Onassis, First Lady, 1929

. . . AND DEATHS

Theodore Roosevelt, president, 1919

Alexander Graham Bell, inventor, 1922

Henry Cabot Lodge, senator, 1924

Woodrow Wilson, president, 1924

Annie Oakley, sharpshooter, 1926

THE WORLD

No war prior to World War I had caused such a terrible loss of human life or destroyed so much property. Modern advances in technology, while generally making peacetime life more pleasant, had also made killing more efficient. Bombs, cannons, and air warfare had rained death on more than 14 million women, children, other non-combatants, and soldiers. After the guns fell silent, anxious people all over the world waited to see whether the Allied victory would truly "make the world safe for democracy." Amidst the ruins, survivors struggled to reestablish some sort of normalcy in their lives.

The Treaty of Versailles, however, was hardly an ideal plan for peace and democracy. It declared the Central Powers—especially Germany—responsible for the war and forced them to pay huge sums in war damages to Allied

AT A GLANCE

▶ **An Old-Style Peace**

▶ **A New World Order**

▶ **The Rise of the USSR**

▶ **The Aftershocks of War in Europe**

▶ **Change in the Middle East**

▶ **Moves Toward Independence**

nations. By parceling out territory of the defeated nations, the treaty drew a new map of Europe but ignored the pleas of many nationalities for self-determination.

Under the harsh peace settlement and its heavy debt, Germany's economy, as well as those of other defeated nations, soon collapsed. Serious problems also arose for the Allied nations of Western Europe who relied on payments from the defeated nations to rebuild their own shattered countries.

The Treaty of Versailles hinted at a new world order by including the League of Nations in its provisions. But the failure of the United States to ratify the treaty and join the League weakened the new organization from the start. In Europe and elsewhere in the world, democracy and dictatorship continued to be at odds, making a lasting world peace seem unlikely.

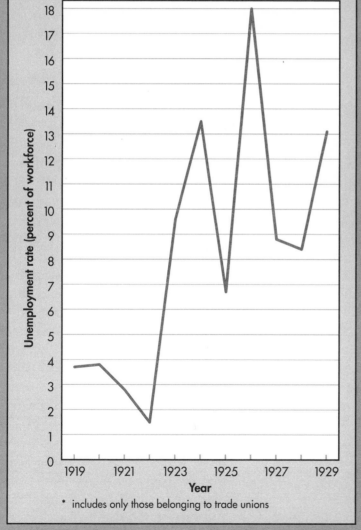

World Population	1920	1930
Total	1.8 bil.	2.1 bil.
Africa	140 mil.	164 mil.
Asia	967 mil.	1.1 bil.
Australia and Oceania	9 mil.	10 mil.
Central and South America	91 mil.	108 mil.
Europe	328 mil.	355 mil.
North America	117 mil.	134 mil.
USSR	158 mil.	179 mil.

A WAR–TORN ECONOMY
Unemployment* in Germany, 1919–1929

Unemployment rate (percent of workforce) vs Year (1919–1929)

* includes only those belonging to trade unions

Source: European Labor Statistics.

AN OLD-STYLE PEACE

In the old days, it was easy to decide how to write a peace treaty after a war. The losers usually had to give up all their lands and possessions to the victors. In some cases, a losing nation disappeared completely and became part of the victor's territory. Or a loser became a colony of the victorious power. The victorious side usually did as it pleased.

"This is a peace conference in which arrangements cannot be made in the old style," declared President Woodrow Wilson as he traveled to the Paris Peace Conference. The Great War, "the war to end all wars," was over. Wilson believed, as did many others, that the old world order was also over and that the guns of war could be silenced forever. Wilson's Fourteen Points gave hope that the nations of the world would work out a "new order of right and justice." President Wilson came to Paris as a messenger of peace with a clear vision of a just and peaceful world and a strong belief that he could make that vision real.

The Fourteen Points

Wilson's views about what was just and peaceful had been stated in his Fourteen Points almost a full year before the end of the war. His principles for world peace included these objectives:

▶ The end of secret treaties and secret discussions between nations.

▶ Freedom for all people to travel the seas in peace and in war.

President Wilson's Fourteen Points represented his attempt to put in place a fair and just peace following World War I. Other world leaders were more intent on punishing the nations that lost the war.

FRANC PROBLEMS

After World War I, France suffered from a rising inflation that brought down the value of the franc, its basic unit of currency. In 1913, the franc had been worth about 20 U.S. cents. By 1926, it had about the same value as 2 U.S. cents. As a result, it was extremely difficult for France to meet its war debts and rebuild its economy.

▶ Removal of all barriers to international trade.

▶ Freedom for all people to decide their own political futures.

▶ Redrawing national boundaries along clearly recognizable lines of nationalities.

▶ Respect for the territorial integrity of other nations.

▶ Formation of an international organization of nations to guarantee world peace by settling disputes.

A peace treaty that followed these democratic principles, Wilson believed, would enable free people to discuss their differences in an atmosphere of trust and cooperation and to create a lasting peace.

The Paris Peace Conference

When the Paris Peace Conference began on January 18, 1919, only delegates from the 27 victorious nations took part. Most of the decisions, however, were made by the Supreme Council, made up of leaders from France, Great Britain, the United States, Italy, and Japan. The leaders of Russia did not attend, because they had signed a separate treaty with Germany after the 1917 Bolshevik Revolution.

At the peacemaking debate, which went on for six months, Wilson tirelessly spoke on behalf of his Fourteen Points. French premier Georges Clemenceau, the "Tiger of France" and chairman of the Supreme Council, had a different point of view. "God gave us his Ten Commandments, and we broke them," he observed. "Wilson gave us his Fourteen Points—we shall see."

Clemenceau doubted that Germany could be trusted to follow democratic principles. Besides, the war had destroyed much of northern France and slaughtered more than a million of its people. Clemenceau wanted the treaty to weaken Germany so much that no German soldier would ever again set foot on French soil. He called for Germany to pay **reparations,** or money for war damages, and to give up large areas of its land.

David Lloyd George, the prime minister of Great Britain, occupied a middle ground between Wilson and Clemenceau. Despite Britain's huge war debts, Lloyd George opposed making Germany pay reparations, knowing that harsh treatment would only anger the German people and plant the seeds for another war. Still he promised the British people he would "squeeze the German lemon till the pips squeak."

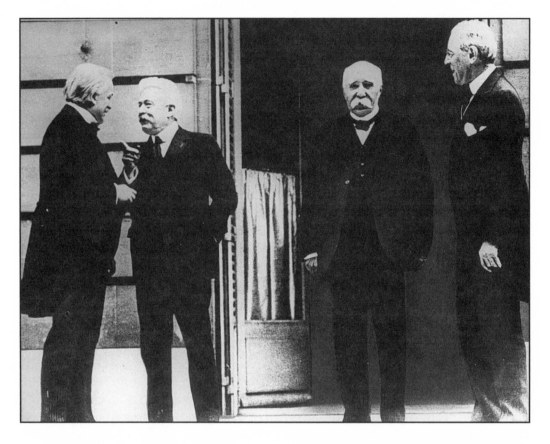

The Italians and the Japanese were more interested in acquiring territory than in assessing reparations. The Italians wanted land that was formerly part of Austria which had been promised them in a 1915 secret treaty in return for joining the Allied war effort. The Japanese wanted the German colonies taken in China and the Pacific.

The Finished Treaty

When the Treaty of Versailles was finally signed on June 28, 1919, it was more a weapon to punish Germany than a blueprint for world peace. Clemenceau got most of his demands for a weakened Germany. Germany was forced to admit total responsibility for the war. It lost Alsace-Lorraine, its colonies in Asia and Africa, and the Rhineland, which was to be administered by the Allies for 15 years. In addition,

Germany had to disarm and pay massive war damages. Italy and Japan received only part of the lands they wanted. Wilson compromised, agreeing to the treaty's requirements to gain support for the League of Nations.

Additional treaties were signed by the other defeated powers. One split up the Ottoman Empire, making many of its former territories in Eastern Europe and Southwest Asia into League of Nation **mandates** under the control of Great Britain and France. Another treaty divided the Austro-Hungarian Empire, making Austria and Hungary separate nations. Seven regions that had been ruled by the former German, Austro-Hungarian, and Russian empires became the free nations of Poland, Yugoslavia, Czechoslovakia, Finland, Estonia, Latvia, and Lithuania.

THE LEAGUE'S COVENANT

The covenant of the League of Nations, which was incorporated into the Treaty of Versailles, was approved on April 28, 1919. The covenant itself had 26 articles. Both the council and the assembly were given the power to discuss "any matter within the sphere of action of the League or affecting the peace of the world." Geneva, Switzerland, became the League's headquarters.

A NEW WORLD ORDER

In the end, conference leaders lost the peace as surely as Germany lost the war. "We arrived at Paris determined that a peace of justice and wisdom should be negotiated," recalled one participant many years later. "We left it knowing that the treaties imposed upon our enemies were neither just nor wise." The Treaty of Versailles was too harsh to allow Germany to join the new world community of free nations, as Wilson wanted. But it was not harsh enough to destroy Germany completely, as Clemenceau wanted.

While the treaty was a disappointment to many people, it provided one of the keys to Wilson's vision of a peaceful world—the League of Nations. The League, Wilson believed, would give world leaders another chance to correct the injustices of the harsh peace treaties and to create a new world order.

The League of Nations

Wilson was put in charge of writing the **covenant** for a League of Nations. The League of Nations had three main bodies—an assembly, a council, and a secretariat. All member nations were represented in an assembly, which met at least once a year. Each nation had one vote, and all decisions had to be unanimous. Most of the League's political work, such as settling international disputes, was done by a smaller body known as the council, whose decisions also had to be unanimous. Practically speaking, these voting requirements made it difficult for the League to agree to act on any matter of importance. The secretariat, made up of an international staff of several hundred officials, administered League activities. The covenant also provided for an International Court of Justice, or World Court.

In one of history's ironies, Wilson's own country refused to ratify the Treaty of Versailles or join the League. Nevertheless, the United States sent representatives to League meetings and cooperated with some League activities, including efforts to reduce arms.

During the 1920s, the League of Nations found peaceful solutions to several minor disputes. The question of whether the League could stop an all-out attack by a major country, however, remained unanswered. The League

Nobel Peace Prize Winners, 1919–1929

1919	Woodrow Wilson	American educator/president of the United States
1920	Léon Bourgeois	French statesman/jurist
1921	Karl Branting Christian Lange	Swedish journalist/politician Norwegian internationalist
1922	Fridtjof Nansen	Norwegian explorer/humanitarian
1923	Not awarded	——
1924	Not awarded	——
1925	J. Austen Chamberlain Charles Dawes	British politician American diplomat/statesman/vice president of the United States
1926	Aristide Briand Gustav Stresemann	French statesman German statesman
1927	Ferdinand Buisson Ludwig Quidde	French educator/peace advocate German pacifist
1928	Not awarded	——
1929	Frank Kellogg	American lawyer/statesman

controlled no troops or weapons, and even its attempt in 1925 to declare offensive war an international crime failed. More successful was the League's efforts to stop the flow of illegal drugs, to improve child welfare and health conditions throughout the world, and to increase international trade. The League also made destroying the weapons of war a primary goal.

The desire of European nations to be protected from another invasion limited the League's willingness to reduce arms. Although the United States never joined the League, it played a key role in all three of the major arms-reduction treaties of the 1920s.

U.S. Moves

In November 1921, the United States invited eight nations to come to Washington, D.C., to discuss the reduction of naval armaments. Charles Evans Hughes, the U.S. secretary of state and leader of the Washington Conference, in a shocking move, asked the participating nations to destroy their battleships. Although the move was not entirely successful, Hughes's bold strategy led to two important agreements.

> *"The height of folly is to imagine that the cutting of armaments would assure world peace. World peace is best maintained when nations are armed to the hilt."*
>
> —Gen. Kenichi Oshimi of Japan, 1923

The League of Nations and the Tragedy of Armenia

The League of Nations heard Armenia's desperate cry for help in 1920 but did nothing to relieve, or remedy, its tragic plight.

In the 1890s, the people of Armenia had suffered violence at the hands of the Ottoman Turks, who had ruled their land for 400 years. The Armenians had tried to defend themselves against the attacks and form an independent nation. Between 1894 and 1896, Ottoman officials had nearly 200,000 Armenians massacred. Although some European leaders expressed concern about the "Armenian question," they took no action.

During World War I, the Turks, who entered the war on the side of Germany, accused the Armenians of fa-voring the Allies, especially the Russians, their traditional rivals. The Turks consequently deported the Armenian people from the land where they had lived for more than 2,000 years, primarily to the deserts of Syria. In the forced relocation process, more than 1 million Armenians died, most of starvation and disease. The Armenians who survived scattered throughout the world.

▼ ▼ ▼

For two years, the Armenians tried to gain international acceptance for their new republic.

Some survivors—perhaps a million—made it to Russian territory, where they established the independent Republic of Armenia in 1918. For two years, the Armenians tried to gain international acceptance of their new republic. They appealed to the League of Nations for recognition, but the League refused to act. Meanwhile, the new republic had to solve serious economic problems and fend off continuing attacks by the Turks, who had reclaimed some land from Armenian control.

In 1920 Turkey threatened to take over all of Armenia. Rather than surrender to Turkey, the Armenians turned over the territory they still controlled to the Bolsheviks in Russia, creating the Soviet Republic of Armenia. In one of its first tests to respect the sovereignty of a nation, the League of Nations had failed.

In a Four-Power Treaty, the United States, Great Britain, Japan, and France agreed to respect each other's possessions in the Pacific and to consult if any nation threatened their Pacific island possessions. Italy then joined these nations in a Five-Power Treaty, which aimed to limit the number of active large warships and to stop the building of new ships. The treaty had little real effect, however, since it never limited smaller ships or submarines.

France, always worried about another German invasion, proposed to the United States that the two nations sign a treaty outlawing war. Frank Kellogg, the U.S. secretary of state, suggested to Aristide Briand, the French foreign minister, that they invite other nations to sign the pledge to settle all disputes peacefully. More than 60 nations signed the treaty, called the Kellogg-Briand Pact (1928). The pact declared war illegal, but it never stated how attackers would be punished. It also did not outlaw defensive wars, leaving a convenient justification available to aggressor nations.

Critics of the Kellogg-Briand Pact said it encouraged people to believe that a "parchment peace" would keep them safe. By the end of the next decade, however, most of the pact's signers were at war.

THE RISE OF THE USSR

By the spring of 1917, the Russian Empire was a powder keg that needed only a spark to set it off. After the revolution of 1905 had been brutally crushed by Czar Nicholas II, the people had waited, silently enduring the czar's harsh rule. When World War I erupted, Russia joined the Allies. By 1917 German forces had plunged deep into Russia. Nine million Russian troops were either dead, wounded, or imprisoned. The rest were tired of war, tired of the czar, and tired of being hungry. The troops were ready to quit.

The Russian Revolutions

In March 1917, women workers from Petrograd's textile district began demonstrating against the conditions in the factories of the czar's regime. Officials ordered

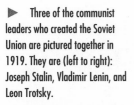

▶ Three of the communist leaders who created the Soviet Union are pictured together in 1919. They are (left to right): Joseph Stalin, Vladimir Lenin, and Leon Trotsky.

troops to disband the crowds. When the troops stood idly by, the revolt spread quickly and resulted in the overthrow of the czar on March 15.

For a few months, the new leaders of Russia—members of the moderate wing of the Socialist Democratic Labor party—tried to establish a democratic government. But they were unable to give the people what they wanted. Soldiers wanted the war to end, workers wanted higher pay to buy food, and peasants wanted their own land to farm.

In November 1917, the radical wing of the party—the Bolsheviks, led by Vladimir Lenin—overthrew

Revolution and Famine: Russia's Time of Suffering

◄ Millions of Russians died and millions more suffered daily from hunger in the famine of 1921–1922.

First came the revolutions of 1917, then the civil war. First Bolshevism, then communism. But always, it was a time for dying. "It loves blood, the Russian earth"—these words penned by the Russian poet Anna Akhmatova voice the misery and anguish felt by the Russian people in the years after World War I.

To the rest of the world, Russia's civil war was a conflict between the communists and those who opposed them. But the civil war soon became Lenin's war against the peasants. This struggle was part of Lenin's plan from the very beginning. The Bolsheviks needed the peasants' help to throw out the landowners and take over the land. "But after that our roads part," Lenin said. "Then we shall have to engage in the most decisive, ruthless struggle against them."

The struggle became increasingly bitter. The central issue in the conflict between the Bolsheviks and the peasants was food. The peasants insisted on their right to sell the grain they had grown. The Bolsheviks, on the other hand, believed the state had the right to seize the grain to use as it wished.

While the battle raged, the fields lay fallow. In 1916, Russian farmers planted 214 million acres of land; six years later, only 133 million acres were under cultivation. Annual fertilizer use dropped from 700,000 to a mere 20,000 tons. Harvests yielded about half the grain they had before the war. The result was predictable, but no one took steps to stop it. A famine swept through the land, reaching its peak in 1921 and 1922.

The human toll of the civil war and the resulting famine was staggering. Nine million people died between 1918 and 1920. About a million were killed in the civil war, and 2 million more died from typhus, cholera, and other diseases. The other 6 million died of starvation or were killed by communists. Five million more Russians died in the great famine of 1921–1922. Many who survived were forced to flee their homes, wandering from one hunger-stricken area to another, from one arena of war to another. For the unfortunate Russian people, it was a time for dying.

► Soviet leader Lenin leads a May Day demonstration.

the moderate wing. Taking over the government, the Bolsheviks vested authority in a "Council of People's Commissars," with Lenin as council chairman. Becoming known as communists, the Bolsheviks promised "Peace, Bread, and Land." Lenin proclaimed, "Long live the revolution of the workers, soldiers, and peasants." To those who opposed him, he shouted, "Go where you ought to be: into the dustbin of history."

"Red" versus "White"

After the Bolshevik Revolution came civil war—three years of bloodshed, misery, and death as the Bolsheviks struggled to stay in power. Lenin faced tough opposition from Russians called "Whites," who opposed communism. Leon Trotsky, Lenin's closest ally and the military leader of the Bolsheviks, organized armies of "Red" workers to fight the Whites, who were helped by Allied arms, supplies, and troops. Yet one by one the Red armies defeated their White opponents. By 1921 the civil

war was over, and Lenin's communists had won.

The takeover by the communists was a tribute to Lenin's masterful strategy and Trotsky's organizational talents. While the Bolsheviks were completely dedicated to their goals, their enemies were disorganized and often squabbled among themselves. The Bolsheviks also did something about the grievances of soldiers, workers, and peasants. They promised soldiers an end to the war. They encouraged workers to establish "soviets" and take over factories. They called on the peasants to take over the property of their landlords.

The New Economic Policy

In 1921 a law was enacted that marked the end of what was called "War Communism" and the beginning of the New Economic Policy (NEP). The NEP combined features of **capitalism** and **socialism.**

At first under War Communism, Lenin tried to build a completely communist state. All factories, mines, and businesses were

THE TREATY OF BREST-LITOVSK

Under this 1918 treaty, Russia lost the Ukraine, Georgia, and Finland to independence. The agreement with Germany forced Russia to give up Poland, the Baltic states, and parts of Belorussia to Germany and Austria-Hungary. It also forced Russia to cede three regions to the Ottoman Empire.

owned and controlled by the government and run by Russian workers. All agricultural land was also owned by the government, and all goods were sold in government-owned stores. But War Communism was unable to meet the needs of the people because, under the Treaty of Brest-Litovsk, Russia had given up a third of its farmland and 90 percent of its coal mines to make peace with Germany. By 1921, food was scarce, people were starving, and the economy was near total collapse.

Under the NEP, some small factories, stores, and businesses could be owned and operated for profit by private citizens. Farmers could sell for their own profit any extra food they were able to grow. These changes provided an incentive to work harder and produce more. Slowly the economic situation in Russia improved.

Socialism in Russia

From the start, Lenin's goal was to use the communist ideas of Karl Marx to build a socialist society. In 1924, after the civil war ended, the communists established the Union of Soviet Socialist Republics. This government was a "socialist" way of organizing the areas that had made up the old Russian Empire. The constitution of the USSR provided for an elected legislature, which chose a council and commissars to rule the Soviet Union. But the constitution looked beyond Russia itself. The founding of the USSR was "a decisive step on the way to uniting the workers of all countries into one World Soviet Socialist Republic," according to the new constitution.

A republic in name only, the USSR was really a dictatorship, completely controlled by Lenin and his handpicked communist associates. The Communist party was the only political organization permitted, and only carefully selected Russians could join. The Communist party itself was controlled by the Central Committee headed by a secretary. Under the new government, the Central Committee and its secretary became the real rulers of the Soviet Union.

When Lenin died in 1924, a four-year struggle for control of the party and the Soviet Union began. Leon Trotsky was Lenin's logical successor, but Joseph Stalin, as the secretary of the Communist party's Central Committee, held the real power in the Soviet Union. Stalin made certain Trotsky would not be able to attend Lenin's funeral. He then used Trotsky's absence as proof that Trotsky did not care about the Communist party or the state. Within a few years, Stalin had exiled Trotsky to Siberia and become dictator of the USSR.

Stalin's New Direction

Stalin turned away from Lenin's drive toward world revolution. Instead, he emphasized "Socialism in One Country." In 1928 he announced the first Five-Year Plan, aiming to turn the Soviet Union into a major industrial power. "We are becoming a country of metal, a country of automobiles, a country of tractors," Stalin proclaimed in 1929.

Stalin's government took over all private farms and businesses. Millions of peasants were forced to

TROTSKY VERSUS STALIN

Stalin exiled Trotsky to Siberia in 1928. One year later he banished Trotsky entirely from Russia. For a time Trotsky lived in Turkey, France, and Norway. In 1937 he settled in Mexico, where he used the press to attack Stalin. Angered over Trotsky's attacks, Stalin had him assassinated in 1940.

move onto **collective farms.** Millions more were forced to move into cities to work in factories. Resisters were starved to death, sent to slave camps, or executed by the secret police—Stalin's new weapon of terror. By the end of the decade, the Five-Year Plan seemed to be working, and the Russian economy did show signs of remarkable progress. The nation had also seen indications, however, of the terrible **purges** that Stalin would inflict on the Soviet people in the years ahead.

THE AFTERSHOCKS OF WAR IN EUROPE

The world had never before suffered a disaster like World War I. Western Europe, where much of the fighting took place, was especially hard hit. Sixty-five million troops fought in the conflict; almost 15 million soldiers and civilians died. Some nations lost almost an entire generation of men. The land suffered too, as battles

Young Joseph Stalin: The Making of a Dictator

Born Joseph Dzhugashvili in 1879, Stalin grew up in the hill town of Gori in the state of Georgia. One of his early teachers described him as unusually vicious, uncommonly skilled at beating up his schoolmates and tormenting teachers, who in turn often beat him as punishment for his bullying.

Stalin's alcoholic father often beat both his wayward son and his wife without mercy. As a result, Stalin as a youth developed a deep hatred for his father, who died in a brawl when the boy was 11 years old.

Stalin's mother never gave up on her son despite his early troubles. As a deeply religious woman, she wanted her son, a great reader of books, to become a priest in the Greek Orthodox church. So, with great hope, she sent him to the seminary at age 15.

There, to her dismay, Stalin continued his rebellious ways. He hated his teachers and was constantly in trouble, often for reading "forbidden" books written by political radicals, such as Karl Marx. After four years, he was ordered to leave the seminary.

By this time, Stalin was convinced of two things: the "truths" asserted by the state and the church were nothing but lies, and the czar could—and should—be overthrown by the people of Russia. He promptly joined the political underground to work toward ousting the czar.

In his work toward a revolution, he joined Lenin's Bolshevik wing of the Social Democratic Labor party. He was jailed seven times in 11 years for various crimes. In 1913, the year he took the name Stalin, meaning "man of steel," he was exiled to Siberia for life. In 1917, he returned to Petrograd to take part in the Bolshevik Revolution. Better educated than his fellow revolutionaries, Stalin became editor of the party's newspaper, *Pravda*, and slowly worked his way up the party's ranks.

and bombs leveled cities, destroyed farms, and polluted farmland.

Recovery from this costly and bitter war was difficult, whether a nation was a winner or a loser. The Treaty of Versailles had carved old empires into many new nations. These nations struggled to write constitutions, form governments, rebuild their economies, and pay their war debts. Even the victors faced huge debts and serious economic problems.

The Money Problem

Debt and **inflation** plagued everyone. Every nation was in debt. Great Britain, for example, owed the United States $4.6 billion in war loans. Great Britain, however, could pay the United States only if France, Italy, and Russia paid back the $6.5 billion they had borrowed from Great Britain during the war. The only hope France and Italy had of paying their debts, in turn, was by collecting reparations from Germany. Germany owed Allied nations a staggering amount— about $35 billion.

As nations struggled to reschedule payments and arrange for new loans, prices plunged and many farms and factories failed. Thousands of farmers and factory workers joined former soldiers in the hunt for scarce jobs. Many Europeans had no money to buy food.

Then prices began to rise— quickly and without letup. In 1918, for example, a visiting American exchanged one U.S. dollar for 14 German marks. By 1923, the exchange rate for a U.S. dollar was 570 million marks. A visiting American congressman paid 1.5 billion marks for dinner in a restaurant, leaving a tip of 400 million marks.

German banks charged 35 percent interest each day on loans but paid 18 percent each year on deposits. So severe was inflation that one peasant woman sold a cow and deposited the money in a bank. Six months later, she took the money out and could only afford to buy a fish. Although Germany suffered more from economic problems than other nations in Western Europe, none escaped.

WAR DEBTS— A VICIOUS CYCLE

During and immediately after World War I, the United States loaned its allies more than $10 billion. Only with timely payment of German reparations, however, could the Allies repay their loans. With the coming of the Great Depression in the 1930s, all reparation payments ceased. Of all the Allied debtor nations, only Finland repaid its entire debt.

New Republics

The Treaty of Versailles had created many new European nations, each free to choose its own form of government. All set up democratic republics.

Some prospered. Czechoslovakia became one of the most democratic nations in Europe. It also became one of Europe's leading industrial powers. Others, such as Austria, survived as republics but remained weak and vulnerable to their stronger neighbors.

Many of the new republics suffered from instability and were not strong enough to resist being overthrown by military leaders who ruled as dictators. Joseph Pilsudski, an army general, seized power in Poland in 1926. Pilsudski ruled Poland as a dictator, even though he once remarked that he got off the streetcar of socialism at the stop called independence. Hungary, after flirting with communist rule, fell to the military dictatorship of Admiral Miklós Horthy. Most of the Balkan republics were also taken over by dictatorships.

Great Britain

The postwar years were difficult for the British people. They had helped win the war, but the sense of triumph faded quickly. Soon after the war ended, Britain's traditional agricultural system collapsed. Huge estates owned for generations by families of the upper class and worked by tenant farmers were broken up into small farms and sold to the highest bidder. As the wealth of the upper class declined, one cabinet minister was led to write, "There is taking place the greatest change which has ever occurred in the history of the land of England since the days of the Norman Conquest."

Britain's industry was also in trouble. The equipment in Britain's coal mines, shipyards, and textile factories—key export industries before and during the war—had become outdated. Unable to compete with more economically produced goods from other nations, factories and mines closed, and many workers lost their jobs.

To protest these conditions, Britain's transport, railway, and mining workers joined in a nationwide general strike in 1926 to protest the loss of jobs. The strike, however, had little effect in slowing the decline of the British economy.

France

France had suffered more direct damage than Great Britain during the war. In fact, the French believed Germany had tried to use World War I to destroy France completely as a major power. But the French rebuilt their factories and farms quickly, in part because they feared Germany would attack once again. "I can tell you," one French official warned, "I look forward with terror to [Germany] making war upon us again in ten years." It took more than ten years, but the attack eventually came.

In politics, the French government suffered from instability. During the years after the war, the lower house of the French legislature forced the prime minister out of office whenever it disagreed with government policies. Many prime ministers remained in office less than six months.

Italy

Italy's problems continued long after the end of World War I. Unemployed former soldiers were unhappy about the lack of jobs, and inflation threatened to destroy the fragile economy. Many Italians felt cheated by the Allies, who had refused to give Italy the Austro-Hungarian lands that had been promised in exchange for entering the war. Frustrated, the Italian people were ready to accept someone they thought could solve their

Eamon De Valera and Irish Independence

"It will be the dawn of a new day for Ireland," Eamon De Valera declared in 1932 when he became prime minister of the Irish Free State. De Valera, an American-born mathematics teacher, led the Irish in their struggle for independence against Great Britain.

Before World War I, most people in Ireland wanted self-government from Great Britain. The Home Rule Bill passed in 1914 granted the Irish some freedom, including their own parliament, but not enough to satisfy the thirst of the Irish Republican Brotherhood for independence. On the day following Easter 1916, the brotherhood led a revolt against British rule known as the Easter Rebellion.

British troops quickly put down the uprising, however, and executed 15 Irish leaders. While the rebellion received little public support, the executions gave rise to great sympathy and outrage. De Valera was one of the rebellion's leaders. For his part, he was at first sentenced to death. His sentence was later changed, and he was imprisoned until 1917. His work for Irish independence continued. De Valera became president of Sinn Fein, an Irish nationalist movement founded in 1905 whose name means "We Ourselves."

After World War I ended, the Irish Republican Army (IRA), which wanted complete independence from Britain, continued to stir up unrest. Many people were killed as the IRA and British troops fought for control of the streets. Meanwhile, the Irish Parliament and the British government looked for a way to end the fighting.

In 1920, the Government of Ireland Act set up separate parliaments for Northern and Southern Ireland. The following year, a new treaty was proposed, giving the Irish Free State (Southern Ireland) freedom to govern itself within the British Commonwealth. Almost immediately, civil war erupted between those Irish people who favored the treaty and those who opposed it. At issue was whether or not anything less than total independence was acceptable. De Valera refused to take the oath of allegiance to Britain required by the treaty and led the opposition to its terms. His forces, however, were defeated in the civil war.

By 1927 De Valera decided he could take the oath after all. His new party, Fianna Fáil, quickly became the largest party in Irish politics. Except for two three-year periods, De Valera served as prime minister of the Irish government from 1932 until 1959. He was also president of Ireland from 1959 to 1973.

► Italian dictator Benito Mussolini used threats of violence to force the king of Italy to appoint him prime minister.

problems. That man was Benito Mussolini.

Mussolini was a journalist-turned-radical who wanted to rebuild the once-mighty Roman Empire. In 1919, Mussolini started the Fascist movement, which he named after the fasces, the Roman symbol of authority. "Believe, Obey, Combat," was the Fascist slogan.

By the fall of 1922, Mussolini's black-shirted troops, using threats and violence, had seized control of a number of Italian cities. "I tell you," he shouted to 6,000 of his followers on October 23, 1922, "either the government will be given to us or we shall take it, descending upon Rome. It is now a question of days, perhaps hours." The black-shirts responded with a single voice, "To Rome!"

The march on Rome and the strength of the Fascist movement forced King Victor Emmanuel III to make Mussolini prime minister of Italy. By 1925, Mussolini had named himself dictator. In the years that followed, Mussolini locked his grip on all Italy.

FASCISM AND MUSSOLINI

Using his system of fascism, Mussolini held tight control over political, economic, religious, and social activities within Italy. Mussolini, who called himself *Il Duce* ("the leader"), might also have been called "two-faced." Before World War I, he was a pacifist and wanted to outlaw war. He was also a socialist. In his rise to power, he abandoned both pacifism and socialism.

Germany

It was a great tragedy that Germany's first experience with democracy came at a time of defeat and misery. Early in 1919, an elected assembly met in Weimar to write a new constitution for Germany. The constitution established the Weimar Republic and gave freedom and the right to vote to all Germans. In June, however, the assembly was forced to accept the Treaty of Versailles and the loss of large amounts of land, people, and natural resources. The treaty also required Germany to pay huge reparations.

Many Germans were angry that their leaders had signed the treaty. They called it a "stab in the back" and accused the leaders of the new republic of treason. Of course, the new government had no choice but to sign the treaty. Nevertheless, communists and other militant minorities threatened to overthrow the Weimar government. In addition, the new republic faced rising unemployment and inflation.

In response, Germany announced in 1922 that it would stop paying reparations. France and Belgium responded by sending troops into the Ruhr, a key factory and mining region of Germany. Ruhr workers went on strike to protest the French occupation, but that only made inflation worse and pushed the economy closer to collapse. The republic seemed ready to fall apart.

It was at this point that a previously obscure politician emerged as the chief spokesman for the National Socialist German Workers' (Nazi) party. Adolf Hitler believed Germany could become powerful once again—with him as dictator. Accompanied by his storm troopers, Hitler tried in 1923 to overthrow the local government of Bavaria in its capital, Munich. He failed and was sent to jail for five years.

The Ruhr crisis ended when an American, Charles G. Dawes, negotiated a plan to reduce Germany's payments and secure more foreign loans. The French and Belgians withdrew their troops. The German economy recovered, and politics settled down. But Hitler, released from prison after only nine months, prepared for a new struggle to win power.

Mein Kampf

Although Adolf Hitler remained in prison for only nine months of his five-year sentence for attempting to overthrow the Bavarian government, he had time to write *Mein Kampf* ("My Struggle"). The book described his vision of Germany's future and his plans to steal land from other nations. In it, Hitler also voiced his hatred of those he considered non-Germans, especially Jews and communists.

When released from prison in 1924, Hitler began the ten-year process of successfully rebuilding the Nazi party. After the Nazis proved the strongest party in the elections of 1932, Hitler was named chancellor.

CHANGE IN THE MIDDLE EAST

For the people of the Middle East, World War I brought secret pacts, broken promises, and shattered dreams. The Arabs in the Middle East wanted independence, and Jews in Palestine and around the world wanted a homeland. The Allies, who needed the help of both Arabs and Jews to win the war against Germany, made promises they could not possibly keep. The result was what has been called "the Palestine Problem"—a stormy legacy of hate and violence.

Too Many Promises

When World War I broke out, the British were in danger of losing their far-flung empire. The Ottoman Turks had joined the **Central Powers,** threatening British lands in the Middle East. In a countermove, the British government made an agreement with

◄ Adolf Hitler (standing) speaks at the founding of the Nazi party. The party promised Germans a return to their nation's past glories.

> Prior to World War I, much of the Middle East was under the control of the Ottoman Turks. Their defeat in the war led to the creation of new nations.

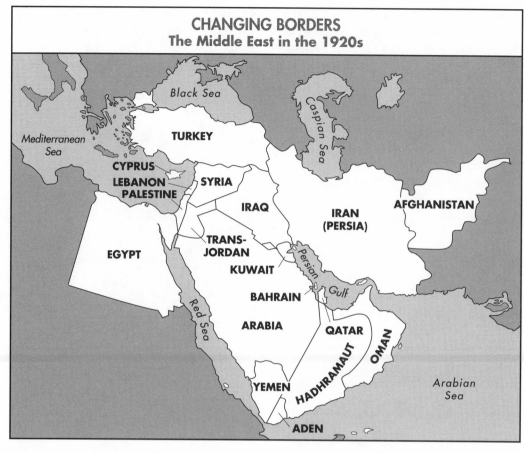

**CHANGING BORDERS
The Middle East in the 1920s**

Sharif Hussein to raise an Arab army and fight the Turks. The British, for their part, promised to support the formation of an independent Arab nation on the Arabian peninsula after the war.

Meanwhile, Great Britain also made a secret deal with France. In the Sykes-Picot Agreement, Britain and France agreed to divide the Ottoman Empire between themselves and Russia, leaving only a part of the Arabian peninsula to the Arabs. To some, the Sykes-Picot Agreement represented a contradiction in British policy; to the Arabs, it was clearly a betrayal—a double cross.

Arab Reaction

The British continued making promises. Long before the war, Jewish leaders of the movement known as **Zionism** appealed to Britain for land in Palestine in order to establish a Jewish nation. Britain offered a homeland for Jews in East Africa, then in Cyprus. Jewish leaders turned down both offers, preferring a Jewish nation in Palestine, the ancient homeland of the Jewish people.

During the war, Dr. Chaim Weizmann was one of the leading Zionists in Britain. Weizmann, a world-renowned chemist, made several important scientific discoveries that helped Britain in the war. He also became friends with Lord Balfour, the British foreign secretary. Weizmann asked Balfour to support the Jewish cause. Balfour recognized Weizmann's request as Britain's chance to strengthen its influence in the Middle East and rally Jews around the world to the Allied cause.

On November 2, 1917, Balfour issued this statement: "His Majesty's Government views with favor the establishment in Palestine of a national home for the Jewish people." Balfour continued by saying that the British government would do everything it could to achieve this goal. In later years, a Jewish leader called the Balfour Declaration "the decisive diplomatic victory of the Jewish people in modern history."

Thirty years later, it led to the founding of the state of Israel, with Weizmann becoming its first president.

When the war ended, Hussein's son Faisal went to the Paris Peace Conference to remind the British government of its promise. Even after the Balfour Declaration, the Arabs had been promised that Jewish settlement in Palestine would not limit the political freedom of the Arabs. Weizmann and the Zionists

Kemal Atatürk: Father of Modern Turkey

By the Treaty of Sèvres (1920), the Allies reduced the once-mighty Ottoman Empire to the Anatolian peninsula, an area also known as Asia Minor, recognizing it by the new name of Turkey but keeping it under control of the Ottoman sultan. Turkish nationalists, however, defied the sultan and the Allies, forming a revolutionary government and army. When the Greeks, with the encouragement of Allied leaders, tried to attack Turkey, the tough- and independence-minded nationalists fought back.

The leader of the nationalists was a seasoned general named Mustafa Kemal. His campaign against the Greeks became the war of Turkish independence. Kemal rallied the Turkish army, pushed the French and Italians out of southern Turkey, pushed the Armenians out of eastern Turkey, then fought the Greeks and their Western allies. The battles were bloody and intense, but the Greeks were not a match for Kemal and his troops.

Now free from foreign threats, the Turks negotiated a new treaty—one that was much kinder to the Turks than the original. They deposed the Ottoman sultan and established a republic. Not surprisingly, Kemal himself led the new government, serving as president until his death in 1938.

According to one account, he "literally ordered his awed countrymen into the twentieth century," in many ways acting as a virtual dictator. For the first time in any Muslim country, Kemal separated church and state. He urged women to put aside their traditional veils and to adopt Western styles of dress, to vote, and to hold public office. He also started a five-year plan to industrialize Turkey's economy with new railroads, factories, and mines.

Kemal was in a hurry to westernize Turkey. In 1928 he ordered the Roman alphabet to replace the traditional Arabic script. He also ordered all Turks 40 years of age and under to go to school to learn the new alphabet. Later, he ordered all Turks to adopt a family name. He himself added the surname *Atatürk*, meaning "Father of Turkey," to *Kemal*, which means "the perfect one."

were in Paris as well. The Zionists wanted the Balfour Declaration made part of the peace treaty. In Weizmann's words, they wanted a nation "which would be as Jewish as the French nation was French and the English nation English."

From the start, the Arabs fared poorly. The Paris Peace Conference created a map of the Middle East along the lines that generally exist today, except for the present-day nation of Israel. Britain was given the mandate to oversee Iraq and Palestine. Although the mandate was temporary, Palestine was at some point to become a homeland for the Jews, and Iraq a fully independent nation. France was given a mandate to oversee what later became the present-day nations of Syria and Lebanon.

Arab Nations Achieve Self-Determination

From the vast Ottoman Empire, many new Arab nations emerged in the 1920s. Three were Saudi Arabia, Egypt, and Iran.

Beginning in 1902, the Saudi leader Ibn Saud led military raids against the Ottoman Turks to regain territory taken by them in the 1800s. After siding with the Allies in World War I, Ibn Saud was rewarded by being granted control over much of the Arabian peninsula. By 1927, he had unified four of the retaken lands and signed a treaty of recognition with Great Britain.

In 1932 Ibn Saud renamed his lands the "Saudi Arabian Kingdom." At that time, no one realized that vast underground pools of oil lay hidden beneath Saudi Arabia's desert sands. As the result of the development of these rich resources, Saudi Arabia is a major power among the nations of today's Middle East—and, indeed, in the world.

Egypt was still a part of the Ottoman Empire when Great Britain declared it a protectorate in the 1880s. Britain wanted to safeguard the Suez Canal, which was vital to British trade.

▼ ▼ ▼

The modern map of the Middle East was largely determined in the years following World War I.

After World War I, Egyptian nationalists began demanding freedom from all British control. In 1922, Britain suspended Egypt's status as a protectorate and gave it independence under the rule of King Fuad I. In 1936 Britain withdrew the last of its military forces.

The monarchy lasted until 1953, when the Egyptian army seized power and established a republic.

The political situation in Persia after World War I was confused, as it had been for some time. During the nine-

teenth century, its ruling dynasty had strengthened ties with Europe, particularly Great Britain and Russia. In an attempt to reject foreign domination, a revolution broke out in 1905 but was foiled.

After World War I, both Great Britain and Russia tried to reestablish their domination of Persia. In the midst of political confusion, Reza Khan, an army officer, led a successful coup and assumed control of the country. In 1925, he named himself shah and assumed the throne as Reza Shah Pahlavi. He also restored the country's ancient name, Iran.

In 1941 British and Soviet troops invaded Iran and forced Reza Shah from the throne. They installed his son, Muhammad Reza Pahlavi, in his place. He ruled until 1979, when Islamic religious leaders led by the Ayatollah Ruhollah Khomeini forced him from the throne and into exile.

The Arab world exploded in anger at what they considered British betrayal. Arabs in Jerusalem attacked Jews in the city. The French used planes and tanks to put down Arab resistance in their Syrian mandate. The violence was most serious in Iraq, where Arab resentment burst into a five-month rebellion against the British that took 130,000 British troops to put down.

By 1920, the British realized they had made a serious mistake. "We are big enough to admit a fault and turn a new page," wrote one British official. In 1921, the British called a conference in Cairo to make another try at settling the Middle East problem. The conference created Transjordan, a new Arab state across the Jordan River from Palestine. The following year, Winston Churchill tried to explain the Balfour Declaration in a new way. The idea, he said, was to create a Jewish home somewhere in Palestine, not to give all of Palestine to the Jews.

A Legacy of Hate

Despite these efforts, the tensions between Arabs and Jews continued to grow steadily. In 1929, a series of clashes occurred between the two groups over claims to the Temple Mount in Jerusalem, a holy place to both Jews and Arabs. Jewish worshipers took benches to sit on at the Wailing Wall, part of the Temple Mount. Several times the police took the benches away, but the Jews kept putting them back. Arabs saw this as a Jewish attempt to strengthen their claim to the Temple Mount. Whipped up to an emotional rage by fanatics, the

Arabs went on a rampage, killing more than 100 Jews and destroying six Jewish settlements.

In the 1930s, Jewish settlers from around the world moved into Palestine. Western nations supported Jewish claims to the land, which increased Arab anger and resentment. Hate and violence, already on the rise, became a trademark of this ancient land.

MOVES TOWARD INDEPENDENCE

While many European nations were struggling to rebuild after the destruction of World War I, a different kind of struggle was taking place in Asia and Africa. People in these regions had long suffered indignities and repression under **colonialism.** After World War I, many were restless. Longing for freedom, many actively began to work for independence.

China

The revolution of 1911 had established a republic in China, but the government was unable to unify the nation. By 1916, local warlords were competing for power, and a period of chaos began that lasted for more than ten years.

One of Wilson's Fourteen Points had urged world leaders to return Shandong province, a former German territory occupied by Japan, to China's control. When the peace treaty gave Shandong to Japan, angry Chinese students took to the streets in a 1919 protest known

AN EARTHQUAKE ROCKS JAPAN

As an island nation, Japan is frequently rocked by earthquakes. Some are only slight tremors, but others have caused severe destruction and loss of life.

On September 1, 1923, the nation suffered its most devastating quake. Almost 60,000 people died in the disaster, which destroyed most of central Tokyo, the nation's capital. Buildings collapsed and fire ravaged the city.

Rebuilding took almost 20 years. During this time, Japan modernized and industrialized, becoming a mighty military nation in the process.

► Chinese leader Jiang Jie-shi was a young man when he led the Nationalists against the warlords of northern China. At first allied with Mao Ze-dong's Communists in the struggle, Jiang parted ways with Mao's forces in the mid-1920s. The two leaders would remain enemies for many years.

as the "May Fourth Movement." "Down with the Traitors!" they shouted. "Return Shandong!"

The May Fourth Movement turned the thinking of many Chinese toward radical solutions to China's problems. Some formed the Chinese Communist party in 1920, with the help of agents from the Soviet Union. On July 21, the first congress of the Communist party was held in secret aboard a ship in Shanghai harbor. Among those present was Mao Ze-dong (Mao Tse-tung), a communist leader from Hunan province.

Sun Yixian (Sun Yat-sen), the founder of the young Chinese Republic, allied his Guomindang (Nationalist party) in 1923 with the newly formed Communist party. For military advice, Sun turned to Jiang Jie-shi (Chiang Kai-shek), who trained officers for the revolution at his base in Guangzhou

province. After Sun's death in 1925, Jiang took control of the Guomindang and launched a military campaign known as the "Northern Expedition" against the warlords. He also turned against the communists. By 1928 Jiang had gained control of most of China, executing many of his enemies, including communists. But Mao Ze-dong and many of his followers escaped execution and retreated into hiding, where they began to organize a revolution that would eventually result in the communist takeover of China.

India

British rule in India was three centuries old by the time World War I ended. During the war, nationalists in India began agitating for self-rule, a goal Britain seemed to agree with in 1917 when Edwin Montague, the secretary of state for India, promised the colony "the gradual development of self-governing institutions."

But the promise went unfulfilled. Instead, in 1918 and 1919, the British Parliament passed the Rowlatt Acts, measures that gave the British officials in India the power to arrest and try in secret any political protestors. The Rowlatt Acts stirred up further unrest. When British troops fired on a peaceful crowd gathered at a walled park in Amritsar to listen to political speeches, killing 400 and wounding 1,200 more, the people were outraged and ready to resist British control.

The nationalist protests continued after the passage of the Montague-Chelmsford Reforms in 1919. As part of these reforms,

Parliament enacted a new constitution for India. The new constitution, however, withheld the promised freedom from British control. As a result, agitation for self-rule continued.

At the Indian National Congress meeting in 1920, Indian leader Mohandas Gandhi presented a proposal for **civil disobedience,** widespread resistance to British rule, but in a nonviolent way. When the congress endorsed the proposal, Gandhi called for a peaceful **boycott** of the British schools, courts, and other official agencies. Students stayed away from classes in government schools, voters stayed away from the polls, and government offices were closed as employees called in sick or resigned. The British, blaming Gandhi for the disruptive boycott, arrested him and sentenced him to prison for six years.

After serving two years, he was released by the British. Then in 1924 Gandhi began a second boycott. This time he urged Indians to become self-sufficient, calling on them to boycott all British-manufactured textiles. To replace the textiles, Gandhi urged everyone to spend time each day at the spinning wheel. He believed that time spent at the wheel would purify hearts and minds for the struggle ahead. The goal of Gandhi's plan was true self-rule for India.

Indians rallied to the new boycott. They wore white "Gandhi caps" as they spread the gospel of nonviolence, literacy, and hygiene. Indian workers went on strike against British companies and formed small cottage industries at home. Throughout the decade, the Ma-

Gandhi's "No, Thank You"

In 1920, Mohandas Gandhi returned three medals awarded him by the British government for his war service and his work for human rights. With the medals, Gandhi enclosed this message: "I can retain neither respect nor affection for a government which has been moving from wrong to wrong to defend its immorality."

hatma ("great-souled"), as Gandhi came to be known, kept the pressure on the British. By the end of the decade, the demand for self-rule under the British flag changed to a demand for complete independence.

Africa

The peace settlement after World War I made some changes to European colonial rule in Africa, mandating Germany's colonies primarily to France and Britain. In the high-sounding words of the League of Nations, the colonies were to be governed as "a sacred trust of civilization," and were to be prepared for economic and political independence some time in the future. In practice, however, Britain and France did little to prepare the people for the future, extracting the wealth of the colonies for their own purposes.

When the first Pan-African Conference had gathered in London in 1900 to discuss the problems that faced African people, leaders asked why Europeans had not provided Africans with more opportunities for education, as many European missionaries had promised. When the second Pan-African Conference was held in 1919, black African leaders asserted their case more strongly. They insisted that the people of Africa must have the right to participate in their own government.

At the same time in America, Marcus Garvey with his "back to Africa" movement was echoing similar sentiments. A month-long convention in New York elected Garvey provisional president of Africa. The title was unrealistic, of course, but pressure for change was growing and some were turning to open rebellion.

In 1921, for example, a Berber chieftain led a revolt against the Spanish rulers of Morocco. After four years of fighting, the chief and his followers were powerful enough to carry the rebellion into French Morocco. Even so, the map of Africa remained almost unchanged until the end of the European empires after World War II.

Latin America's New Stance

Most nations of Latin America did not take an active part in World War I. Only eight, including Brazil, Costa Rica, and Panama, declared war on Germany. Five broke off relations with Germany. Mexico, Argentina, and five other nations remained neutral.

Many Latin Americans were interested in the outcome of the war, however, especially immigrants from Spain, Portugal, Italy, and Germany. In addition, many Latin American nations relied on British markets for their agricultural exports. As a result, they anxiously awaited the war's outcome.

With the Allied victory and the powerful contributions of the United States to it, Latin American nations shifted their focus away from Europe and toward their powerful neighbor to the north and the postwar economic boom it was enjoying. American business leaders headed south, searching for new markets for their goods and new supplies of raw materials.

In many ways, the 1920s were a continuation of the pre-war policy in Latin America called "dollar diplomacy." The U.S. government used its influence to protect and extend American business interests. By 1924, for example, the United States had control over financial policies in 14 out of 20 Latin American nations.

At times, American presidents sent American troops to intervene in the affairs of Latin American nations to keep the goods and dollars flowing. For example, the U.S. military occupied Nicaragua in 1912, staying for 13 years until President Calvin Coolidge withdrew the soldiers in 1925. Once the American troops withdrew, however, a revolt led by anti-American rebel César Augusto Sandino threatened to take over the pro-American government.

In 1926, Coolidge sent in the Marines once again. Some members of Congress criticized the president for interfering with

NICARAGUA

Over the years, Nicaragua has experienced many changes in leadership and various forms of intervention by the United States government. U.S. Marines first landed in Nicaragua in 1912 at the request of the elected president to stop a revolt against him.

For the next 20 years, American military forces remained in Nicaragua. Rebels led by General César Augusto Sandino engaged them in guerrilla warfare from 1927 until 1933, when U.S. troops were again withdrawn. The next year Sandino was murdered by members of the Nicaraguan National Guard.

Nicaragua's internal affairs. The president's response was that the United States was not making war on Nicaragua any more than a police officer on the street is making war on people who walk by.

In 1928 U.S. policy toward Latin America began to change when leaders from many Pan-American nations met in Havana, Cuba, to discuss regional issues. The United States was criticized for its role in Latin America. One Latin American leader emphasized that the United States must respect the freedom of other nations to conduct their own affairs. American leaders began to realize that to people in other nations soldiers were not seen as agents of good. Although many nations welcomed foreign businesses, few greeted foreign troops with open arms.

By the end of 1928, U.S. military forces had withdrawn from Cuba, the Dominican Republic, and Nicaragua. Dwight Morrow, the American ambassador to Mex-

ico, helped ease tensions between the United States and its neighbor to the south over rights to Mexican oil. Morrow's mission to Mexico set in motion a new era of cooperation.

Between Herbert Hoover's election as president in November 1928 and his inauguration in March 1929, the president-elect made a goodwill trip to Latin America. As Hoover traveled through the region, he made frequent use of the term "good neighbor." In Uruguay, he declared, "I have hoped that I might by this visit symbolize the courtesy of a call from one good neighbor to another, that I might convey the respect, esteem and desire for intellectual and spiritual cooperation."

Four years later, President Franklin Delano Roosevelt borrowed Hoover's expression for use in his inaugural address. "I would dedicate this nation to the policy of the Good Neighbor," he said. A new era in relations with Latin America had arrived.

BUSINESS AND ECONOMY

After a brief postwar slump, the American economy began seven years of spectacular, if uneven, growth unlike any in its history. Many Americans had money to spend and an exciting selection of new products to buy. The technology of mass production enabled factories to churn out an endless stream of cars and new consumer goods—at prices the average worker could afford to pay.

The construction business also enjoyed a boom, as companies used their profits to erect higher and higher buildings, skyscraping monuments to their economic success. The stock market soared sky-high as well. Some investors were lucky enough to turn small sums into vast fortunes almost overnight. For many in the upper and middle classes, it was an era of easy money and easy living.

AT A GLANCE

▶ **Economic Ups and Downs**

▶ **Keys to Prosperity**

▶ **A Consumer Era**

▶ **The Automotive Age**

▶ **Signs of Weakness**

Unfortunately, most farmers, blue-collar workers, and blacks did not share in the nation's overall prosperity. Crop prices remained depressed throughout the decade because farmers were able to grow more food than the nation needed. Blue-collar workers, both whites and blacks, in the mining, steel, and textile industries also struggled to make a living.

Consumer spending during the 1920s nevertheless pushed the economy to its highest limits. The prosperity, however, quickly disappeared when the supply of consumer goods began to exceed demand for them and too many purchases were made on credit. When the economy ran out of fuel, the stage was set for a disastrous crash and a long, hard depression.

DATAFILE

Wealth and productivity	1919	1929
Gross national product	$84.0 bil.	$103.1 bil.
Per-capita income	$619.00	$705.00
Trade balance		
Imports	$5.9 bil.	$5.9 bil.
Exports	$10.8 bil.	$7.0 bil.
Dow-Jones average	119.62	381.17
Raw steel output (short tons)	38.1 mil.	61.7 mil.
Auto factory sales	1.6 mil.	4.5 mil.

Labor force	1919	1929
Total	40.3 mil. (1920)	48.8 mil. (1930)
Male	79.6%	78.1%
Female	20.4%	21.9%
Unemployment rate	1.4%	3.2%
Union membership	4.1 mil.	3.4 mil.

Government	1919	1929
Federal spending	$18.5 bil.	$3.1 bil.
National debt (−) or surplus (+)	−$13.4 bil.	+$734.4 mil.

MARKET BASKET
Retail Prices of Selected Items, 1924

 Bread (1 lb.): **$0.09**

 Milk (½ gal., delivered): **$0.27**

 Woman's dress: **$22.00**

 Man's suit: **$55.00**

 Postage (1st class, 1 oz.): **$0.02**

 Three-minute phone call (New York to Denver): **$7.25** (1926)

 Car (Chrysler): **$1,395.00**

 Movie ticket: **$0.15**

 Victrola: **$137.50**

 Electricity (per kilowatt hour): **$0.03** (1922)

ECONOMIC UPS AND DOWNS

Most economists agree that, over several decades, the economy of a nation moves through several stages in a process known as a **business cycle.** Every period of expansion, or prosperity, is followed by a period of **recession** when profits slump, sales fall off, and unemployment increases. The period of recession may be caused by a crisis, such as a stock market crash. Or it may gradually develop into a slow downturn. Depending on its length and severity, a recession may be called a depression. The years immediately before, during, and after the 1920s are a perfect example of the business cycle and its stages.

A Slow Start

The United States fought World War I as much with its farms and industry as with its military. "It is not an army that we must train for war," proclaimed President Wilson, "it is a nation." Under the guidance of the War Industries Board, factory and farm production rose to record levels. The Fuel Administration convinced people to conserve precious fuel through "heatless Mondays" and "lightless nights." Under Herbert Hoover, the Food Administration mobilized the nation to create less waste and more production.

When World War I ended, however, the economy began to slip into a recession for a variety of reasons. For one, in 1919, the War Industries Board, which had controlled production and prices, ended its direction of the U.S. economy. The government also stopped subsidizing prices for crops and certain industrial goods. At the same time, overseas demand for these items dropped. As a result, farm prices fell and the stock market slumped. Some companies went out of business, and many returning veterans could not find jobs. In parts of the United States, strikes by blue-collar workers demanding wage increases were common. In 1922, the economy hit a low point, but it soon began to recover.

With the exception of two brief downturns, the nation enjoyed a period of recovery, economic growth, and prosperity from 1922 to 1928. Industrial production, corporate profits, and personal income rose, reaching record levels. Some people spoke of an economic boom. Others talked about a business fever sweeping the nation. Still others spoke of the period as the "Roaring Twenties," in tribute

to a roaring economy. Whether a boom, a fever, or a roar, and regardless of what fueled prosperity, everyone agreed that, generally speaking, the period was one of great economic expansion.

Economic Expansion

During the Roaring Twenties, Harding, Coolidge, and Hoover occupied the presidency. All were Republicans, and all were former businessmen. All believed in laissez-faire, an economic philosophy that said the federal government should give big business freedom to expand and prosper. With freedom from regulation by government, they believed that all Americans would reap the rewards of a healthy economy.

Accordingly, the Republican presidents moved to cut taxes on corporations and wealthy individuals. They took steps to slow the labor union movement. They also appointed business leaders to key government positions and eased up on regulation of industries. "Never before, here or anywhere else, has a government so completely fused with business," observed the *Wall Street Journal.*

The Workforce

During the 1920s, large corporations with specialized managers dominated the mass production of automobiles and new consumer goods. Workers in these industries shared in the prosperity. Aided by an increase in wages, blue-collar workers had more money to spend. With an increase of service and office jobs, white-collar workers moved into the middle class. In contrast, blue-collar workers in

▼ Miners walk away from their jobs at the start of a coal strike. Most strikes during the 1920s were unsuccessful, and union membership fell.

steel, textile, mining, and other older industries barely made a living. In general, organized labor fared badly in both established industries and new corporations, mainly because of the government's probusiness bias.

In 1919, 350,000 steelworkers went on strike for higher wages and a shorter workday. When their demands were rejected, a series of violent and bloody conflicts erupted from Pennsylvania to West Virginia, the heart of the nation's steel industry. The same year coal miners began a year-long strike, and their campaign was just as unsuccessful. In both cases, business owners, taking advantage of the "Red Scare" of the early 1920s, accused union leaders of being communists and trying to start a "Red" revolt. The tactic worked. Unions quickly lost public support. Membership in labor unions dropped from 5 million to less than 3.5 million.

Corporate leaders also tried to reduce the influence of unions, taking advantage of several key Supreme Court rulings limiting workers' rights to protest. By the late 1920s, the Ford Motor Company employed a private security force of about 8,000, mostly former convicts. These "hired guns" successfully discouraged union activity in Ford's factories.

A more positive way for business leaders to keep their workers from joining unions was to keep them happy. To this end, many employers improved working conditions. They hired company physicians and dentists to provide health and dental services at reduced prices. Some employers also

Black Labor Organizer A. Philip Randolph

Asa Philip Randolph, the son of a Methodist minister, moved to New York City from the South at 17. He took a job as a busboy and elevator operator by day and studied college courses at City College by night. In the *Messenger* magazine and on the streets of Harlem, where he preached black activism, Randolph often urged blacks to take action against those who treated them unjustly.

His commitment to the cause of black equality met its stiffest test in 1925 when a group of black porters who worked on the sleeping cars of the Pullman Company on long-distance trains asked for his help. They described the low pay and terrible working conditions they had to endure. In response to their complaints, Randolph organized the porters into a labor union, the Brotherhood of Sleeping Car Porters. The *Messenger*, a socialist magazine for blacks that Randolph had helped found in 1917, became the official magazine of the new union. With Randolph's quiet but determined leadership, the Brotherhood won its fight to bargain with the railroads on behalf of its members.

In 1929, the Brotherhood of Sleeping Car Porters, with Randolph as its president, became part of the American Federation of Labor (AFL). Randolph eventually became a vice president of the combined AFL-CIO.

His greatest contributions, however, came as a leader of the black struggle against injustice. They included his pushing President Franklin D. Roosevelt toward the creation of the Fair Employment Practices Committee to protect the rights of blacks in industry and government. Randolph also directed the historic March on Washington for Jobs and Freedom in 1963.

provided recreational activities. Others sold their employees cheap gasoline, constructed "company towns," and paid for many other benefits. U.S. Steel alone spent more than $10 million a year in its employee benefits program.

Still other companies gave workers a voice in corporate management. Business owners argued that cooperation between employers and employees, which was often called "industrial democracy," was good for everyone. They reasoned that "those who really know each other cannot fight." For the most part, owners were successful in their tactics. By 1929, only one worker in eight belonged to an independent labor union.

Women continued to be a part of the corporate workforce during the 1920s. The female workforce outside the home, however, increased by only 27 percent during the decade. By 1930, almost half of all women employed outside the home worked at white-collar jobs.

Most women worked at such relatively unskilled jobs as typists, clerks in stores and offices, telephone operators, and cashiers. Few advanced into management positions, meeting with sex discrimination when it came to promotions and their acceptance in the workplace by males.

As Sinclair Lewis wrote in a book called *The Job*, women were "expected to keep clean and be quick-moving; beyond that they were as unimportant to the larger phases of office politics as frogs to a summer hotel."

Big business ruled the work world during the Roaring Twenties. Labor unions and women had a place in this world, but it was small and carefully controlled. As long as profits kept rolling in, any calls for change went unheeded.

Commerce

KEYS TO PROSPERITY

Several developments keyed the economic expansion of the 1920s. One was the probusiness stance of the Republican presidents who led the nation during the 1920s. This favorable environment sped the growth of large corporations and their domination of the economy. Another factor was new management techniques. Still another key was the technological advances that increased productivity.

Corporate Growth

During the 1920s, the size of businesses expanded along with the economy. Large corporations

▼ Women were an important, if underappreciated, part of the workforce during the 1920s. Many, such as these telephone operators, worked in the few fields considered appropriate for women. These tended to be low-paying clerical positions, such as secretary or cashier.

dominated the economy. By 1929 half of America's corporate wealth belonged to 200 of the nation's largest corporations.

Efficient Management

Large corporate empires required new management techniques and a new breed of managers. Undergraduate students began asking for courses and majors in business, commerce, economics, and marketing. Leading universities and colleges established business schools and granted both undergraduate and graduate degrees in marketing and business administration. They also set up special classes and workshops to train corporate employees to be executives, supervisors, and managers in charge of such special departments as sales, advertising, accounting, and personnel.

Increasing Productivity

Another key to the prosperity of the 1920s was the advances in technology that increased productivity. Assembly lines and electric-powered machines became common. Between 1914 and 1929, for example, the use of electric-powered machines rose 40 percent. The increased use of electric-powered machines caused a rising demand for electric power. Since some electricity was generated by oil and natural gas, the petroleum industry in California, Texas, and Oklahoma began to grow.

With advances in technology, the same number of workers who made 100 radios a day in 1922 made 170 radios a day in 1928. Overall, technology led to a 50 percent rise in productivity during the 1920s.

Industrial Growth

"All you have to do is plug it into an electric outlet . . . and then you can forget it," promised a magazine ad for electric refrigerators. The 1920s were a golden age for American consumers. Factories mass-produced electric refrigerators, radios, phonographs, and other new or improved consumer goods designed to make life easier and more enjoyable.

Relatively new industries, such as automobiles and motion pictures, took their place alongside established industries. The growth of the automotive industry spurred growth in other established industries, creating a demand for vast quantities of steel, rubber, glass, and textiles. Service stations popped up everywhere, ready to refuel and repair the nation's automobiles and trucks.

The Booming Stock Market

Perhaps nothing captures the spirit of the Roaring Twenties better than the spectacular growth of the stock market. The decade was a time when many people thought everyone could become rich, but it was also a time of excessive profits and uncontrolled greed. One politician promised, "If a man saves $15 a week, and invests in good common stocks . . . at the end of twenty years he will have at least $80,000 and an income from investments of around $400 a month. He will be rich."

Market trends seemed to support the search for riches. By mid-decade, a million and a half Americans owned active stock market accounts. The **Dow-Jones industrial average,** the average price of

> "*We* in America today are nearer to the final triumph over poverty than ever before in the history of any land. The poor-house is vanishing from among us."
>
> —Herbert Hoover, 1928

TOP TEN INDUSTRIAL COMPANIES, 1925

1. U.S. Steel
2. Bethlehem Steel
3. General Motors
4. Armour & Co.
5. General Electric
6. Swift & Co.
7. DuPont de Nemours
8. International Harvester
9. Allied Chemical
10. American Tobacco

▲ The volatile stock market turned Wall Street into a turbulent place during the 1920s.

in Liberty Bonds to help finance the war. A popular jingle of the day summed up the spirit of the times:

> My Tuesdays are meatless,
> My Wednesdays are wheatless,
> I'm getting more eatless each day.
> My coffee is sweetless,
> My bed it is sheetless,
> All sent to the YMCA.

After several years of conservation and scarcity, the response of American consumers to the prosperity of the 1920s was an enthusiasm for consumption—for fulfilling their needs and wants.

Higher Incomes

The dawn of the consumer era came when three things happened at more or less the same time. First, people began to earn more money. For example, in 1914 Henry Ford established the $5 workday, an increase of $2 a day over prevailing factory wages. Later Ford raised the minimum wage in his factories to $7 a day. Between 1923 and 1929, the average income of American workers increased 11 percent. Although the increase was small in terms of actual dollars, prices remained stable. As a result, Americans had more buying power. This buying power enabled them to purchase the things they needed in order to survive and still have money left to spend on luxuries.

New Products

Just as workers had more money to spend, a vast range of new consumer products appeared in the stores. The new electric refrigerators kept food fresh more conveniently than had the iceboxes of the past. Americans enjoyed the

30 major stocks, rose from 64 in 1921 to 200 in 1927. In the next 21 months, the price of many stocks more than doubled.

Economic expansion, in some respects, was a reaction by American consumers to the difficult times they had experienced during World War I. They worked from dawn to dusk on farms and in factories to support the war effort. They conserved fuel and electricity, and they tried to "Use All Leftovers" and "Serve Just Enough," as the patriotic slogans of the Food Administration requested. If patriotic Americans had any money left at the end of the month, they invested

BIG BANK ERA

The National City Bank in New York City was the first bank with resources exceeding $1 billion. On November 17, 1919, this bank, which later evolved to the current Citibank, had assets totaling $1,027,938,114.31.

happy alliance of two great conveniences, uniformly sliced bread and the electric toaster. Housewives gloried in such electric appliances as irons, vacuum cleaners, and washing machines, although these appliances did not necessarily leave them with more leisure time. Instead, the new gadgets took the place of housemaids, washer women, and cleaning women, often leaving housewives with less help and more work to do for themselves.

Lower Prices

Advances in the technology of mass production drove down the cost of manufacturing goods, resulting in savings to the consumer. A Model T car, for example, cost $850 in 1908, but only $290 in 1927—less than two months' income for the average middle-class white family. As prices dropped, even those who could little afford to buy the new appliances found the lure of "buying on time" too enticing to hold back.

Installment Plans

Despite higher wages and lower prices, few American families were able to pay the lump sum of $97.50 for a washing machine or $28.95 for a vacuum cleaner. To overcome this obstacle, stores and manufacturers came up with installment plans, a way of "enjoying while you pay." Instead of $97.50, the cost of a new washing machine became "$5 down, $8 a month." Suddenly, consumer items that were once out of reach became affordable.

Buying on the installment plan, called buying on credit, had its hidden costs. It often added as

Some day you'll buy her a Frigidaire

why not for Christmas

Of course, she wants Frigidaire! And some day you'll buy it. So why not make that *some day* now?

Give her a Frigidaire for Christmas.

Give her the convenience of making desserts with the famous Frigidaire "Cold Control." Give her the care-free, healthful refrigeration assured by Frigidaire's surplus power. Give her the advantages of self-sealing freezing trays that permit two widely different temperatures in the same cabinet at the same time.

In other words, give her a *real* Frigidaire . . . one with the Frigidaire name-plate on it. Then you'll be *sure* she'll have a truly *modern* electric refrigerator. She'll have a cabinet of striking beauty in Tu-Tone Porcelain-on-steel. She'll have the incredible quietness of the Frigidaire power unit . . . a unit that is out of sight and away from dust and dirt. And she'll have the convenient arrangement of the Frigidaire shelves . . . shelves placed at a height that makes stooping unnecessary.

And it's *easy* to give her a Frigidaire. Prices are low and terms can be arranged to suit your convenience. So, avoid the usual last-minute rush. Call at the nearest Frigidaire display room and have Frigidaire in your home on Christmas morning. Frigidaire Corporation, Subsidiary of General Motors Corporation, Dayton, Ohio.

FRIGIDAIRE
More than a MILLION *in use*

▲ The refrigerator was just one of the new appliances and other conveniences sold to the willing public during the 1920s. Purchased in great numbers, they rapidly changed the lifestyles of millions of Americans, many of whom purchased them on credit.

much as 40 percent to the total cost of an item. Even so, many people saw credit as a way to raise their standard of living. Between 1920 and 1929, credit purchases increased fourfold to $6 billion a year. By the end of the decade, 60 percent of auto sales, 70 percent of furniture sales, 80 percent of refrigerator, radio, and vacuum cleaner sales, and 90 percent of piano, washing machine, and sewing machine sales were on credit.

Some people voiced alarm at this trend, warning about the dangers of too much credit. Some economists insisted that credit was one of the driving forces of prosperity. Never say a family has

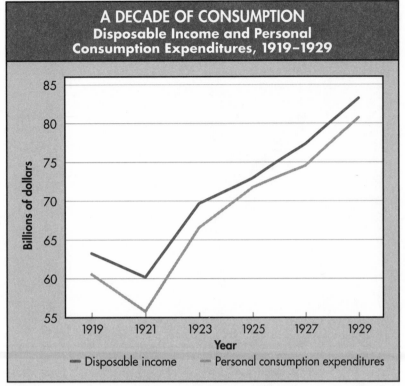

A DECADE OF CONSUMPTION
Disposable Income and Personal Consumption Expenditures, 1919–1929

Billions of dollars (y-axis: 55, 60, 65, 70, 75, 80, 85)

Year (x-axis: 1919, 1921, 1923, 1925, 1927, 1929)

— Disposable income   — Personal consumption expenditures

Source: U.S. Bureau of Economic Analysis.

▲ The rise in spending on consumer goods was a direct result of the fact that most Americans had more money available for that purpose. Disposable income is that which is left after the basic necessities of life have been paid for.

large debts, they suggested; rather, refer to its good line of credit.

Most people did not dwell on the problems credit could cause. They simply kept buying and made jokes about all the "easy little payments" they had to make. "I just paid the doctor another ten dollars on his bill," a husband reportedly told his wife. "Good," she replied. "Only two more payments and the baby is ours."

An Advertising Age

While money and mass production were both vital to the consumer boom, so was advertising. Even thrifty President Coolidge recognized the role of advertising in making "new thoughts, new desires, and new actions" seem attractive to the buying public. "It is the most potent influence in adopting, and changing the habits and modes of life, affecting what we eat, what we wear, and the work and play of the whole nation," he said.

Some advertisements welcomed consumers into a world of luxury and pleasure. "You, too, can have a skin you love to touch," promised the makers of Woodbury's Facial Soap. Would-be buyers of a Jordan Motor Car were told they would "start for the land of real living with the spirit of the lass who rides, lean and rangy, into the red horizon of a Wyoming twilight." One ad proclaimed that Lucky Strike cigarettes protected the throat, stopping smokers from coughing. Another boasted that 45,512 doctors approved their mouthwash. Sex appeal, social snobbery, fear, invented scientific details, and outrageous claims—advertisers used all these tricks and more to convince people to buy, buy, buy.

Before long, it became clear that advertising was a key to business success. By mid-decade, 70 percent of newspaper and magazine income came from advertising. In fact, Americans spent more money on advertising than on education during the 1920s.

Most people credit Bruce Barton with starting the advertising boom. The son of a Tennessee preacher, he founded an advertising agency and became famous for his ability to write effective advertising copy. Barton also wrote a best-selling book, *The Man Nobody Knows*, which said that Jesus was the world's greatest salesperson and the great advertiser of his day.

The stories Jesus told, according to Barton, illustrate the four key principles of advertising: ads must be brief, simple, sincere, and repeated over and over. "No important truth can be impressed upon the minds of any large number of people by being said only once," insisted Barton.

The world created by advertisements, however, was make believe. All too soon, Americans would be forced to face the realities underlying the economy.

▲ Advertisers of the 1920s were free to make product claims that would not be allowed today.

THE AUTOMOTIVE AGE

Will Rogers, the famous American humorist, offered this view to the man who had made the U.S. automotive industry: "So good luck, Mr. Ford. It will take a hundred years to tell whether you have helped us or hurt us, but you certainly didn't leave us like you found us."

Rogers was right. The automobile created a revolution in American society. This revolution transformed the nation forever from one of scattered rural hamlets to one of

The Mass Retailing Revolution

Before the days of mass production, workers in small shops produced a few items at a time. At the corner store, people bought what they needed for the day's meals. In the modern, mass-production world of the 1920s, however, merchandisers needed to sell a high volume of goods.

New types of stores were needed to sell goods as quickly as factories could produce them. During the 1920s, giant retail firms set up thousands of chain stores across the country. The Great Atlantic and Pacific Tea Co. (A&P) chain of grocery stores, for example, had more than 15,000 stores nationwide by the end of the decade. Standard Oil of New Jersey increased its service stations from 12 in 1920 to 1,000 in 1929. J.C. Penney, Sears and Roebuck, Woolworth, and many other retailers spread 160,000 chain stores across the nation by 1929.

▼ ▼ ▼

The rise of the chain stores changed forever the shopping habits of American consumers.

With high-volume buying, or mass retailing, these nationwide chains were able to offer consumers lower prices, wider selection, and better service than the "Ma and Pa" grocery on the corner. American consumers liked the savings of mass retailing, and they flocked to the new chain stores.

Piggly Wiggly took mass retailing one step further. In 1920 this chain of grocery stores introduced "scientific merchandising." Every store was laid out to make use of Piggly Wiggly's unique self-service plan and its patented customer traffic pattern.

People liked being able to choose what they wanted from the many well-stocked shelves of these first supermarkets. By 1929, Piggly Wiggly had 2,500 stores and the highest per-customer sales average in the nation.

MISSING MARQUES

While the auto industry grew rapidly, the number of manufacturers dropped by more than half in the 1920s.

bustling hubs of an urban center ringed by suburbs and tied together by ever-expanding ribbons of concrete.

An Industrial Explosion

The automotive industry experienced a staggering growth. The number of cars registered in the United States jumped from 8 million in 1920 to 23 million in 1929. Almost half a million Americans worked in auto factories by the end of the decade, and countless more workers sold, repaired, and refueled automobiles, trucks, and other gasoline-powered vehicles. Americans, on average, spent one out of every five dollars to buy and maintain their vehicles.

With such growth, the automotive industry became America's largest—a position it still occupies. In addition, the industry became the largest customer in the nation for steel, lead, rubber, glass, nickel, gasoline, and other petroleum by-products. Autos needed good roads, so building roads also became a boom industry. At the end of World War I, the nation had only 7,000

miles of paved roads. Nine years later, there were 50,000 miles of paved roads, with 10,000 miles more being added each year. The automotive industry also supported the 121,500 service stations that lined the new roadways by 1929.

The explosive increase in automobiles and other motor vehicles on the nation's highways not only changed America, but also the automotive industry itself. When the decade began, 100 automotive companies were making vehicles. Some companies went out of business, unable to turn a profit in such a highly competitive marketplace. Others were bought out by more successful companies. In 1925, for example, Walter P. Chrysler took over the Overland and Maxwell companies and created the Chrysler Corporation. Three years later, he acquired Dodge. By the end of the decade, the number of auto companies had shrunk to 44. The industry was dominated by the Big Three—General Motors, Chrysler, and Ford.

One of the leaders of the auto industry was Henry Ford, whose

▶ The rapid growth of the automobile industry was responsible for a boom in associated businesses. One was the building of roads. The nation's highways expanded at a furious pace during the Roaring Twenties.

affordable Model T came in any color, he boasted, "so long as it is black." But competition from Chrysler and other automotive corporations prompted many Americans to look for more variety in colors and models. They wanted their cars to come in colors like Arabian Sand and Versailles Violet. They also wanted closed tops, powerful engines, and the newest safety features. Even Henry Ford was forced to change to meet the public's automotive tastes. In 1928 Ford introduced its new Model A with significant new features. A worthy successor to the Model T, it came in a variety of colors and 17 body styles.

A Social Revolution

"Why on earth do you need to study what's changing this country?" asked a resident of the Midwest during the 1920s. "I can tell you what's happening in just four letters: A-U-T-O." The impact of the automobile on middle-class American social life was just as dramatic as its impact on the economy. The automobile created the greatest revolution in American life ever caused by a single factor.

The privacy offered by the new covered models changed dating styles. The automobile sent people exploring new sights on Sunday outings. When vacation time came,

Alfred P. Sloan: A New Kind of Automaker

Unlike automaker Henry Ford, who as a "self-made" business leader learned from the "school of hard knocks,"

Alfred Sloan was a graduate of the Massachusetts Institute of Technology. After receiving his diploma in 1895, Sloan became employed as a draftsman for the Hyatt Roller Bearing Company. Six years later, he was its president. In 1916, Sloan sold the company to General Motors (GM), becoming its president in 1923.

Unlike Henry Ford, who wanted to build a simple, reliable car almost everyone could afford, Sloan wanted to build and sell a car "for every purse and purpose."

While Ford's genius lay in the way he went about building his car, Sloan's genius lay in the way he built GM. Unlike Ford, who offered everyone the same car,

Sloan offered people a choice from seven different car lines, ranging from a four-cylinder Chevrolet for $795 to an eight-cylinder Cadillac for $5,690.

To manage the production of his cars, Sloan split GM into several divisions, each with its own line of cars. At the same time, he maintained central financial control over all the divisions.

Under Sloan's direction, the automaker grew rapidly to become the largest corporation of any kind in the world. Watching Sloan's success, Ford was forced to abandon his one-car approach and eventually followed Sloan's example of setting up divisions, each with its own line of cars.

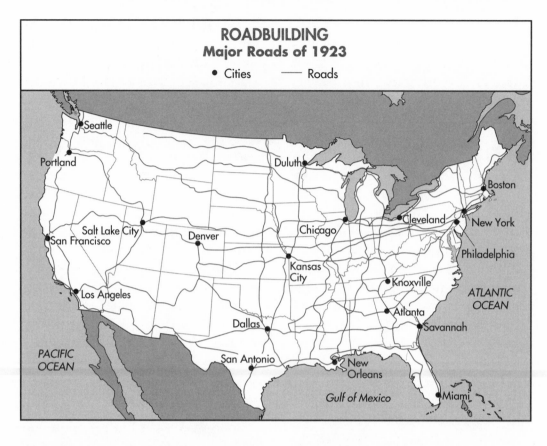

ROADBUILDING
Major Roads of 1923

● Cities —— Roads

Businessman John Hertz worked hard to become the king of taxicabs as founder of the Yellow Cab Company of Chicago. Realizing that people did not always need both car and driver, Hertz started a car rental company—"The Yellow Drive-It-Yourself System, Inc." With the new business venture, Hertz established branch offices across the country where anyone with a driver's license could rent a car.

Hertz based the charges for his rental cars on the type of car rented and the number of miles each customer drove. A Ford touring car, for example, cost only 12 cents a mile, while a closed car went for 22 cents a mile.

families took to the roads to discover the four corners of America and all places in between. The automobile caused the dramatic growth of the suburbs, and it enabled workers to commute to their jobs from homes in "bedroom communities" surrounding central cities and industrial centers. In one short generation, Americans went from poking along in horse-drawn carriages to sitting in traffic jams.

Even as the automobile gave Americans the freedom to roam, it saddled them with debt. "The ease with which a car can be purchased on the time-payment plan is all too easy a road to ruin," wrote one man. "But—I still drive one myself," he continued. "I must keep up with the procession." During the decade, Americans had fallen in love with the automobile, and their love affair revolutionized American social life. That love affair continues today.

Economy

SIGNS OF WEAKNESS

Prosperity, expansion, and technological improvement seemed never-ending to many Americans, even those in high places. Still, signs of weakness in the economic might of the nation were there for observant people to notice. The prosperity of the 1920s never lightened the burdens of many American households. Most farmers, blacks in the South, and blue-collar workers never experienced prosperity, only glimpsing it from afar. Warning signs were also present on Wall Street and in the boardrooms of corporations. They also reached to the White House. Few people in the street and few of the nation's leaders were alert enough, however, to predict the sudden onset or the severity of the event known as the Great Depression.

The Farming Crisis

Many Americans struggled through hard times during World War I, then relaxed to enjoy the prosperity of the 1920s. For farmers, the opposite occurred: they experienced prosperity during the high-demand times of the war and hardship during the 1920s. During the war years, the demand for food skyrocketed, and farmers expanded their acreage to grow more. Their crops brought high prices, which were backed by the federal government in order to keep up production.

With the end of the war, the government ended its price supports, and foreign nations no longer needed to import grain and other foodstuffs. Suddenly warehouses and grain elevators were filled to capacity and prices tumbled.

A bushel of corn brought a farmer enough money to buy 5 gallons of gasoline in 1919 . By 1921, a bushel of corn brought enough money to buy only half a gallon. In farmhouses across the land, a mournful refrain echoed: "No use talkin', any man's beat, with 'leven-cent cotton and forty-cent meat."

Technological advances and other efficiencies also produced farm surpluses. With Henry Ford's gasoline-powered Fordson tractor, a farmer was able to farm larger tracts of land while using fewer hired hands.

Although farmers traditionally opposed government intervention, their situation was desperate. With no relief in sight, they formed the American Farm Bureau Federation and appealed to Congress for help. Sympathetic senators and representatives pushed through the Mc-Nary-Haugen Bill. This piece of legislation called for the government to buy up surplus crops and sell them to foreign countries. Backers of the bill thought it would stabilize crop prices and give farmers enough income to survive. But President Coolidge vetoed the bill. So Congress passed it again, but again Coolidge rejected it. Help for farmers would not come until a Democrat was in the White House.

By the time Hoover became president in 1929, one farm in four had been sold to pay off debts or taxes. To enable farmers to help themselves, Congress passed and Hoover signed the Agricultural Marketing Act. This act set up a

▼ Farmers were not among those who benefited from the business climate of the 1920s. After World War I, which had created great demand for their crops, their income dropped dramatically. Despite some recovery during the decade, agriculture never reached the income levels of 1919 and 1920.

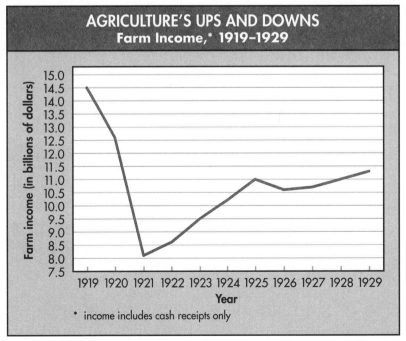

AGRICULTURE'S UPS AND DOWNS
Farm Income,* 1919–1929

Farm income (in billions of dollars)

* income includes cash receipts only

Source: U.S. Department of Agriculture.

Federal Farm Board, which loaned money to farmers' cooperatives so they could buy, sell, and store surplus crops. The Agricultural Marketing Act helped to steady crop prices but did not help them rise.

The Stormy Stock Market

Many people, both then and now, think of the Great Depression as a stray meteor from a distant galaxy that, by unlucky chance, came crashing down to end the prosperity of the Roaring Twenties. Nothing was further from the truth. Rather, the economic collapse was the final stage of a hidden disease that had been eating away at the health of the economy for many years, especially in the stock market.

Much of the great expansion of the stock market was fueled by speculators who bought their stocks on margin, hoping to get rich. Buying stocks on margin was really buying stocks on credit, a practice followed by some Americans. Speculators buying on margin bought stocks by putting down as little as 5 percent of a stock's purchase price.

A speculator, for example, who bought $100,000 worth of stocks, paying the broker $5,000, actually owed the broker $95,000. If the stock doubled and the speculator sold it, the speculator's take was $200,000. With the $200,000, the speculator paid back the $95,000 loan and gained $100,000 on the original stake of $5,000. But a stock price sometimes slid. If its original purchase price dropped by half, the speculator still owed the broker $95,000 but the stock was worth only $50,000, leaving the speculator unable to pay the balance owed. Buying on margin was a main cause of the stock market crash of 1929; speculative balloons eventually burst.

Another factor related to the stock market contributed to the crash. U.S. banks and other investors, flush with cash during the 1920s, made large loans to help foreign governments and corporations rebuild after the war.

Late in the decade, however, investors, instead of banking their profits, began pouring their money into the stock market. Without capital, banks had no money to make new loans. Without loans, other nations could not afford to buy American products. A high protective tax also hindered trade with other nations, increasing agricultural and industrial surpluses. Many businesses slumped in the face of declining demand.

With decreasing sales, production slowed down and unemployment rose. Speculators in the stock market were unable to pay their margin accounts when brokers demanded payment. Excess production, high protective tariffs, easy-credit policies—all contributed to the crash of 1929 and the depression that followed.

Before and After the Crash of 1929

SELECTED STOCK PRICES

	Sept. 5, 1928	Sept. 9, 1929	Nov. 11, 1929
Eastman Kodak	$184\frac{5}{8}$	$214\frac{3}{4}$	$174\frac{3}{4}$
General Electric	166	391	$208\frac{1}{2}$
General Motors	$203\frac{1}{4}$	$71\frac{3}{4}$	$39\frac{3}{8}$
IBM	130	$241\frac{3}{4}$	$139\frac{3}{8}$
U.S. Steel	$153\frac{3}{8}$	$257\frac{5}{8}$	$163\frac{1}{4}$

The Crash

By the summer of 1929, the buying frenzy on Wall Street had been under way for roughly two years. **Speculation** on the stock market had pushed share prices to new heights, but speculators had borrowed $6 billion from their brokers to do it.

A few wary investors began to notice signs of broad economic decline. They saw that construction starts were down, industrial production was dropping, and auto sales were in a slump. Suspecting that the stock market may have reached its peak, these investors sold their shares. Others soon followed. Slowly stock prices began to slide.

The decline accelerated when the British raised their interest rates to lure back investors who had been attracted by the rising profits to be made on the speculative American stock market. By now, brokers in the United States became concerned about marginal accounts, suspecting that many Americans did not have enough cash to pay back their loans. They began to demand repayment, forcing people to sell their stocks, often at a loss.

On "Black Thursday," October 29, 1929, stock prices on the New York Stock Exchange plunged steeply. Panic reigned on Wall Street, as frantic brokers bellowed offers to sell cheap. But few could afford to buy, and prices fell even further. In less than three weeks, stocks lost 40 percent of their total value—a drop of $30 billion. (In the next three years, they would lose another $45 billion.) The stock of one company, Union Cigar, dropped

◀ Even *Variety*, the show business newspaper, took note of the Wall Street crash of 1929. Its headline, however, makes the stock market collapse sound like a box office flop on Broadway. The real effect of the crash was much more serious.

from $113.50 a share to just $4 in one day.

Many people, including President Hoover, thought the stock market and the economy would recover quickly. Andrew Mellon, the secretary of the treasury, said he saw nothing in the stock market crash to cause alarm. Hoover, trying to reassure Americans, said: "The fundamental business of the country, that is, production and distribution of commodities, is on a sound and prosperous basis."

As it turned out, both Mellon and Hoover were wrong. All the signs had been there to see for a long time. Factories and farmers were overproducing. The stock market had been expanding on borrowed money and borrowed time for many months. The nation's economy was being drowned in a sea of plenty, pulled under by a huge weight of debt. The long and painful depression had begun.

GUIDE DOGS

The first dogs trained in the United States to guide the blind were taught at The Seeing Eye, Inc., which was founded by Dorothy Harrison Eustis in 1929. The Seeing Eye, Inc., was first incorporated in Nashville, Tennessee. In 1932, it moved to Morristown, New Jersey, where it still operates.

SCIENCE AND TECHNOLOGY

As the 1920s began, the pace of life was getting faster. Much of the speed was coming from new technological developments and refinements, particularly in the fields of transportation and communication.

Automobiles streamed off the rapidly moving assembly lines to waiting consumers. The new cars were not just faster, they were bigger, better, and, often, cheaper. The decade saw the automotive industry grow quickly to become the nation's largest industry.

Airplanes began to show their promise for commercial transportation. Planes flew faster and farther and carried heavier loads. Due to these improvements, the first passenger airlines were created, hinting at future possibilities for routine, high-speed, long-distance travel.

Radio's potential as an instant communications medium was realized at this time. Using

AT A GLANCE

- ▶ Time-Saving Techniques
- ▶ The Airplane Industry Takes Off
- ▶ The Broadcasting Boom
- ▶ The Discovery of Insulin and Penicillin
- ▶ The Mystery of Matter
- ▶ The Scopes Trial

electromagnetic waves to transmit signals, radio brought the sounds of live entertainment, sports, and news directly into people's homes for the first time.

Medical advances during the decade promised speeded recovery from illness and disease. Physicists continued to probe the mystery of matter, uncovering principles that would lead to practical applications in the future.

While many believed that science was improving their lives, others were not as certain that the rapid change was for the better. For many, Darwin's theory of evolution was the perfect example of science gone haywire. They believed his theory contradicted the truths expressed in the Bible.

The traditionalists were to have their day in court, however. In Dayton, Tennessee, in 1925, modern science went on trial.

DATAFILE

Science

Life expectancy at birth (yrs.)	1919	1929
Males	53.5	55.8
Females	56.0	58.7

Top five causes of death, 1919–1929
1. Heart and kidney diseases 2. Influenza and pneumonia
3. Tuberculosis 4. Cancer 5. Diseases of the intestinal tract

Technology

Miles of paved roads

1919 350,000   1929 662,000

Passenger miles traveled, 1929
Rail .... 31.2 bil.   Air .... 104.0 mil. (1930)

Tallest building in U.S., 1929
Woolworth Building (completed 1913): New York City, 60 stories, 800 ft.

Households in 1920 with . . .

Electricity	35%
Telephone	35%

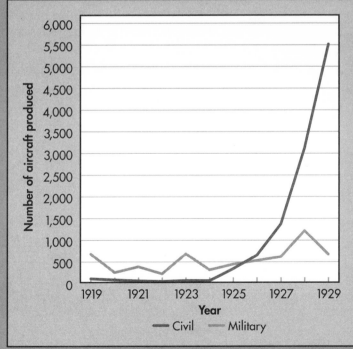

THROUGH THE ROOF
Civil and Military Aircraft Production, 1919–1929

Source: U.S. Federal Aviation Administration.

Manufacturing

TIME-SAVING TECHNIQUES

In 1896 Henry Ford, using technical know-how and a large measure of inventiveness, built his first gasoline engine at home. Twelve years later, the first Model T rolled out of a new Ford automobile assembly factory. Ford, however, wanted more. He wanted to find a way to mass-produce the Model T, so he could sell more cars at lower prices.

The Moving Assembly Line

One day, while touring a meat-packing plant in Chicago, Ford noticed a moving overhead trolley that carried the sides of beef from one worker to the next. Ford saw that the work came to the worker. The moving beef line saved time and increased efficiency because each butcher performed only one task. Ford realized he had found the key to mass production.

Back at his auto plant, Ford started by setting up a moving assembly line to build magnetos, devices that generated current for Model T ignitions. Ford assigned individual tasks to workers lined up along the conveyor belt; this achieved astounding results. It took only five minutes to build a magneto instead of the usual 18. Soon Ford used moving assembly lines to build the entire car. Production tripled between 1912 and 1915, and by the mid-1920s, Ford's plant turned out 2 million new cars each year. Ford's moving assembly line started a revolution in the automotive industry. Some even called the breakthrough a "second industrial revolution."

During the decade, Ford and other automakers perfected the system. Each part of a car was made in huge quantities to precise standards, making the parts inter-changeable. The main systems of the car—engine, transmission, and chassis—were put together on smaller assembly lines that fed into the main line. Workers per-formed their assigned tasks over and over again. For example, one operator of a double drill press drilled a pair of holes in the front ends of three cars per minute. In a nine-hour day, he performed his job 1,620 times.

Ford's new system made work-ers as interchangeable as the parts of the automobile. Nonetheless, workers were attracted to the robot-like jobs because of Ford's intro-duction of the "five-dollar day." The new wage rate came at a time when most employers considered $2 a generous day's wage. In 1926, Ford cut the workweek at his plant from 48 hours in six days to 40 hours over five days. He also raised wages. As a result of good wages and shorter working hours, his plant never lacked workers—no matter how boring and tedious the jobs.

Household Appliances

During the years after World War I, electricity became available to homes in many parts of the United States for the first time. Engineers also perfected a compact electric motor. As a result of these develop-ments and the spread of mass-pro-duction techniques, affordable household appliances began to come off factory assembly lines by the thousands. Vacuum cleaners, washing machines, refrigerators, electric irons, sewing machines, automatic toasters, fans, radios, phonographs—the list was almost as long as an assembly line in a Ford plant.

Traffic and Engineering

Despite a few dips in factory sales, yearly auto production more than doubled in the 1920s. New routes had to be created to handle automobile traffic. New York drivers waited in line for the opening of the Holland Tunnel, the world's first automobile tunnel, on November 13, 1927. It connected New York and New Jersey under the Hudson River. The heavy traffic on its opening day was both a sign of the times and a glimpse of the future in the auto age.

AN INDUSTRY GROWS UP
Passenger Car Factory Sales, 1919-1929

Source: Automobile Manufacturers Association.

The new appliances had a dramatic impact on home life. Radios and phonograph players became fixtures in the average American home, and communication was speeded by the increased use of the telephone.

Affordable, mass-produced furniture, clothing, and other household goods led to a new level of consumption. People did not seem to mind that everyone's cars, clothes, and furniture looked the same. Consumer goods were part of the good life, and everyone wanted a fair share.

THE AIRPLANE INDUSTRY TAKES OFF

If God had wanted human beings to fly, he would have given them wings, many people said about the newfangled machines that were so successful in World War I. The wartime pilots were brave and dashing heroes. Their airborne dogfights with the enemy were spectacular. But many people questioned how useful airplanes could be in peacetime.

Barnstorming

The pilots were determined to find peaceful uses for their flying machines. They longed to push in the throttle and pull back the stick once again, launching themselves and their flimsy planes into the air. Their desire led to adventure. Some bought surplus warplanes and began "barnstorming," flying from

one rural locale to another. At county fairs and wherever else they could draw a crowd, they performed stunts, stood on wings, and gave rides—"Five Dollars for Five Minutes." More than 10 million Americans first learned the thrill of flying in the front seat of a war-surplus Jenny trainer. Even more saw their first airplane when a barnstormer visited their town.

Flying the Mail

Other pilots began flying the U.S. mail. It was a hazardous way to make a living. Of the first 40 pilots to fly the mail between New York and Chicago, 31 lost their lives in crashes. Yet by 1923, pilots were flying mail from coast to coast. As the airmail service became more reliable and dependable, Americans could see that airplanes would be an important part of the growing nation's future.

Coast to Coast

Advances in structural design, aerodynamics, and the mechanisms of control made flying safer and more enjoyable. Techniques were also developed during the 1920s that led to the manufacture of all-metal aircraft bodies. The Ford Motor Company built an enclosed plane, the Ford Trimotor, formed Stout Air Lines, and began offering passenger service.

"Those who hesitate to employ the airplane," one of Ford's advertisements read, "will do well to recall that there are still many old-timers who refuse to ride in automobiles!" By 1929, the time to travel coast to coast had been reduced to 48 hours using a combination of planes and trains.

INVENTIONS, 1919–1929

Electric razor, 1917
Push-button elevator, 1922
Frozen food, 1924
Circuit breaker, 1925
Aerosol spray, 1926
Iron lung, 1928
Teletype, 1928
Electroencephalograph (EEG), 1929

AVIATION CRUSADER

Brigadier General William L. "Billy" Mitchell organized and commanded U.S. air efforts in World War I. After the war, he staged aerial bombings of target ships in order to convince his military superiors that air power had a future in America's defenses.

Mitchell's methods caused a terrible stir. His superiors tried and convicted him of insubordination.

The court-martial, however, captured the public's imagination. In the opinion of one magazine editor, Mitchell did "more for the cause of aviation than any other man in the nation's history except the Wright brothers."

► An exhausted Charles Lindbergh stands in front of the *Spirit of St. Louis* at Le Bourget airport, May 21, 1927. Lucky Lindy's transatlantic flight of about 3,600 miles took him over Nova Scotia, Newfoundland, and Ireland.

Aviation Firsts

Charles Lindbergh, an airmail pilot, dreamed of being the first person to fly across the Atlantic alone, without stopping. To accomplish the task, he designed and had built a special plane. Among other features, it was capable of holding 425 gallons of fuel for the long journey. Carrying five sandwiches and two canteens of water, he took off from New York's Roosevelt Field on May 20, 1927, aboard the *Spirit of St. Louis.* He was bound for Europe.

Thirty-three and a half hours later, Lindbergh landed before a madly cheering crowd at Le Bourget airfield in Paris. The first person to survive a nonstop flight across the Atlantic, he earned a $25,000 prize and became a world hero. He soon became known as the "Lone Eagle."

Writing later of his achievement, Lindbergh said: "No man before me had commanded such freedom of movement over earth. For me the *Spirit of St. Louis* was a lens focused on the future, a forerunner of mechanisms that would conquer time and space."

While Lindbergh's solo flight was the most famous of the decade, other aviators were making history throughout the twenties. One was Richard E. Byrd, who in May 1926 commanded a flight over the North Pole in a Ford Trimotor. Though his nose and fingers were frozen by the icy temperature in the cockpit, Byrd pushed on and confirmed the accuracy of Admiral Robert Peary's earlier observations on the location of the North Pole. For his feat, Byrd was later awarded the Congressional Medal of Honor. In 1929,

► Rear Admiral Richard E. Byrd and his crew prepare their plane, the *Floyd Bennett,* for a flight to the South Pole.

Byrd and three companions flew to the South Pole and, for the first time in history, sent a message by radio from there.

Another pioneer was the Norwegian explorer Roald Amundsen, who reached the North Pole in a **dirigible,** the *Norge.* The May 12, 1926, edition of the *New York Times* announced his latest accomplishment in a headline that read: THE *NORGE* FLIES OVER NORTH POLE AT 1 A.M.; REPORTS FEAT TO *TIMES* BY WIRELESS; GOING ON OVER ARCTIC WASTES TO ALASKA. Amundsen's was the first such message ever transmitted from the North Pole.

Robert Goddard achieved another kind of first flight on March 16, 1926, when he launched the world's first liquid-propelled rocket into the air. The rocket reached a top speed of 60 miles per hour, but it rose only to an altitude of 41 feet before landing 184 feet from the launch stand. From this humble start came the liquid-fueled rockets that would one day make space travel possible.

◄ The American physicist Robert Goddard stands with the world's first liquid-propelled rocket at Auburn, Massachusetts.

Communications

THE BROADCASTING BOOM

In 1916, two decades after the Italian Guglielmo Marconi invented the radio, a 25-year-old wireless operator named David Sarnoff wrote to his boss at the Marconi Wireless Telegraph Company. Sarnoff suggested: "I have in mind a plan . . . that would make radio a household utility. The idea is to bring music into the home by wireless."

At the time, the wireless, as the radio was commonly called, was mainly used to transmit messages by Morse code. Only a few dedicated hobbyists used their microphones and receivers to transmit messages by voice. Their instruments were crude crystal sets, often put together at home out of copper wire and cardboard cereal cartons. At the time only a few unrehearsed talks and music from phonograph records filled the airwaves of "voice radio."

Radio Comes of Age

To put his plan into action, Sarnoff had to wait until 1919, when the government lifted a wartime ban on nonmilitary broadcasts. When the Radio Corporation of America (RCA) took over the Marconi firm in 1920, Sarnoff became its general manager. RCA soon began mass production of its "radio music boxes," followed by Westinghouse in 1921.

RADIO PIONEER

Born in Russia, David Sarnoff came to the United States in 1901 at the age of ten. By the time he was 15, he was working for New York's Commercial Cable Company. Six years later, he was an operator for Marconi Wireless Telegraph Company. While Sarnoff was at work at the telegraph station one night in 1912, a message that the *Titanic* was sinking arrived. For 72 hours, Sarnoff directed rescuers to the ship.

▲ Westinghouse engineer Frank Conrad began broadcasting from his garage in Pittsburgh in 1919. Conrad's hobby turned into Westinghouse's station KDKA, which began scheduled broadcasts in 1920. Later in the decade, William S. Paley (right, standing) hooked up CBS, his network of radio stations.

Consumer demand for radios rose rapidly. In 1920, radio sales totaled only $2 million. By 1922, more than 2 million homes in the nation had radios. By mid-decade, the radio audience in the United States reached 50 million. By 1929, Americans spent $600 million a year on radios, buying everything from build-it-yourself mail-order kits to $50 Crosley sets and more expensive console models. Without a doubt, radios were the most successful consumer products introduced in the 1920s.

Early Programs

The huge demand for radios was created by the rapid increase in radio broadcasts, many sponsored by manufacturers of radio equipment. The first regular licensed broadcasting began in 1920, when station KDKA in Pittsburgh announced the news of Harding's landslide defeat of Cox in the presidential election on November 2. In the lulls between election returns, the station played records, and two banjo players strummed tunes. The program was a tremendous

success. Other types of programs followed, including church services and musical programs.

By 1921 radio had become the fastest-growing industry in the nation. Newspaper owners and other business people wanted to own radio stations. By 1924 there were almost 600 stations across the nation. The airwaves were so jammed with signals that the government was forced to create the Federal Radio Commission in 1927 to assign frequencies to radio stations. Later, the agency changed its name to the Federal Communications Commission.

At first, radio programs were considered a commercial-free public service. One magazine for the advertising business declared, "Any attempt to make radio an advertising medium would, we think, prove positively offensive to great numbers of people." It did not take long, however, for advertisers to change their minds. In 1922, the first paid radio commercial was broadcast in New York City over station WEAF. The commercial cost $50 for 10 minutes. When WEAF made a profit of $150,000 in

1923, the future course of radio was clear.

Radio Networks

By 1926, David Sarnoff, who had become the head of RCA, had another revolutionary idea. He decided to form a nationwide network of radio stations. Under Sarnoff's guidance, RCA bought WEAF and used it as the core of a new network, the National Broadcasting Company (NBC). NBC's first coast-to-coast broadcast brought the Rose Bowl game from Pasadena, California, into millions of American homes on January 1, 1927.

In 1928, William Paley bought the Columbia Broadcasting Company and merged it with a group of smaller companies, forming the Columbia Broadcasting System (CBS). By the end of 1929, CBS had 47 affiliate stations.

Medicine

THE DISCOVERY OF INSULIN AND PENICILLIN

The 1920s saw remarkable gains in public health. New hospitals and improved public sanitation, although concentrated in the cities, helped many Americans stay healthier and live longer. In addition, doctors began to use improved surgical techniques they

RADIO'S VICTIM

The introduction of radio changed Americans' home entertainment habits. One victim of the new medium was the piano-producing industry, which saw sales drop by two-thirds between 1923 and 1929.

The Unearthing of Tut's Tomb

In 1922 the British archaeologist Howard Carter discovered the tomb of the ancient Egyptian king Tutankhamen, commonly referred to as King Tut. Carter had been searching for Tut's tomb for ten years.

When it was entered in 1923, the tomb was found to contain more than 5,000 well-preserved objects, many of which were beautifully carved and formed. They included figures of animals and gods, toys, weapons, and jewelry, much of it made of gold—and all of it more than 3,000 years old. An elaborate throne and coffin were also found.

Carter (in pith helmet) is shown here at the entrance to the tomb with his financial sponsor, Lord Carnarvon (facing camera). Both became famous as their remarkable discovery captured the public's imagination.

had learned treating World War I soldiers. They referred to this new approach as plastic surgery, and it soon became a rapidly expanding field of medicine. Other advances occurred in the treatment of diseases.

Frederick Banting worked on his father's farm in Ontario until he was 19. He entered the Canadian army and served as a battalion surgeon in World War I. After he was wounded, he returned to Canada and became a medical researcher. In 1922, while studying how the pancreas releases fluids into the bloodstream, he and medical student Charles Best first isolated the hormone called insulin. This hormone, they learned, helps the body control the levels of sugar and starch in the blood.

Insulin was a giant advance in the fight against diabetes, a disease that prevents the body from breaking down sugar and starch. Banting and Best's great discovery meant that insulin could be taken from animal tissues and given to

▶ Alexander Fleming's discovery of penicillin was the result of an amazing—and fortunate—series of events. The rare penicillin mold invaded a bacteria culture dish that was left on a workbench while Fleming was on vacation. During this time, the weather turned cold, which encouraged the penicillin to grow. These chance conditions—and Fleming's curiosity—led to the accidental discovery.

people with diabetes. "Insulin, perhaps the most widely heralded discovery of the past year, continues to show promise," *Time* magazine reported in 1923. Banting was awarded the 1923 Nobel Prize in medicine.

A Matter of Luck

Alexander Fleming's discovery of penicillin took place at a London hospital in 1928. A Scottish bacteriologist, Fleming was trying to find a cure for deadly infectious diseases. As he worked, he had a habit of leaving bacteria to grow for a week or two after he finished with them, just to see what would happen. On the day of his discovery, he noticed the bacteria on one plate had been killed by a green mold. Fleming called the mold "penicillin," the first **antibiotic** drug.

Fleming credited his discovery to his work habits. As he studied bacteria, he kept his laboratory cluttered with equipment and culture samples. "Had my lab been as up-to-date as those I have visited," he later observed, "it is possible that I would never have run across penicillin." Unfortunately, Fleming failed to follow up on the possibilities of his own chance discovery. While he continued to use penicillin for his own laboratory purposes, he apparently believed it unimpressive or unpromising as a medicinal germ killer.

Luckily, two chemists, Howard Florey and Ernst Chain, realized the potential of the new substance. It was their work that proved penicillin's value as a drug. For their accomplishment, they were awarded along with Fleming the 1945 Nobel Prize in medicine.

Penicillin has since been used effectively for a wide variety of infectious diseases and has saved many lives. It created a worldwide revolution in modern medicine, giving rise to an entire new family of germ-fighting drugs.

Physics

THE MYSTERY OF MATTER

In the early 1900s scientists continued to peer deeper and deeper into the fundamental nature of matter itself. Researchers found a new way of explaining the basic building blocks of the universe, quantum mechanics.

Before quantum mechanics, scientists had relied on Isaac Newton's explanation of matter. According to Newton, all matter had energy, which it gained or lost in a steady stream. Newton said that the energy level of a specific object rose and fell as though the object were going up or down a ramp. He maintained that matter and its energy could be measured precisely. He also said that future energy levels could be predicted accurately.

As twentieth-century scientists Max Planck, Niels Bohr, and Werner

The Uncertainty Concerning Uncertainty

In 1927, the world's leading physicists met in Brussels for a conference, the Solvay Congress. Both Albert Einstein, who developed the theory of **relativity,** and Niels Bohr, who had developed a new interpretation of the atom based on quantum mechanics, attended the meeting. Their dispute over the theory of quantum mechanics became the talk of the physics world.

Einstein refused to believe the uncertainty principle, one of the cornerstones of quantum mechanics. This principle says that we can never be certain what is happening within an atom, particularly with its electrons. Each day Einstein presented his friend Bohr with an idea for an experiment that could,

in theory at least, disprove the uncertainty principle. Every evening, Bohr would respond by showing Einstein a flaw in his thinking.

▼ ▼ ▼

"Science without religion is lame; religion without science is blind."

—Albert Einstein

At the Solvay Congress of 1930, Einstein greeted Bohr with a new experiment, which Bohr agreed was "a serious challenge." Night came, and Bohr had no reply. Unable to sleep, Bohr continued to wrestle with the problem. As dawn broke, Bohr suddenly saw a key error in Einstein's logic, and once again Einstein's challenge failed.

The dispute was more about philosophy and religion than about science. Einstein believed uncertainty was merely a characteristic of human knowledge, not of matter itself. He believed that as knowledge advanced, it would be possible for scientists to describe with certainty the basic characteristics of matter.

Einstein believed that events in the world were not random. "God does not play dice with the universe," he insisted. Bohr responded, "Stop telling God what to do!" Einstein was never able to disprove the uncertainty principle, nor was Bohr ever able to shake Einstein's belief that the universe is, at its most basic level, orderly and predictable.

Heisenberg studied the atom and its particles, they discovered that energy traveled in packets called "quanta." They found that objects gained and lost energy in jumps, as though the object were going up or down a staircase. These scientists also determined that individual events within an atom were somewhat random and unpredictable.

Newton was mistaken about energy because he lacked the techniques to look at matter closely enough. Examined with better tools, Newton's continuous "ramp" of energy revealed itself to be a "staircase" of unconnected leaps instead. The formulation of quantum mechanics called into question the idea of scientific certainty.

While the new way of looking at matter shook the world of science, it also had many practical applications. Scientists later used quantum mechanics to build lasers and solid-state electronic equipment. It also helped them unleash the energy of the atom, contributing to both the atomic bomb and the generation of electricity through nuclear energy.

The New Galaxies of Astronomer Edwin Hubble

During his college years at the University of Chicago, astronomer Edwin Hubble excelled as a heavyweight boxer. He went on to earn a law degree at Oxford and worked as a lawyer for a short time, before earning a Ph.D. in astronomy in 1917. During the 1920s, this former boxer delivered a knockout blow to the traditional view of the universe.

▼ ▼ ▼

Hubble gathered evidence that the galaxies were moving away from each other.

Soon after Albert Einstein proposed his general theory of relativity in 1916, a Dutch astronomer suggested that the universe might be expanding in all directions. Both these theories excited Hubble, who used the telescopes of California's Mount Wilson observatory to look into the heavens for evidence that would support them.

In 1923, Hubble determined that the universe was composed of many galaxies, not just one huge galaxy, as previously thought. He discovered that the clouds of gas and dust on the fringes of our galaxy—the Milky Way—were actually faraway galaxies, as large as our own. By 1929 Hubble had gathered proof that the galaxies were moving away from each other, as if the universe were actually expanding.

Hubble also made another key contribution to astronomy. In 1925, he set up a system for classifying the galaxies in the universe—the same system that is used today. Hubble's major accomplishments were honored when the National Aeronautics and Space Administration named the first space telescope after him. The Hubble Space Telescope was lifted into orbit by the U.S. space shuttle in 1990.

Evolution

THE SCOPES TRIAL

At first glance, it was a simple court case. In 1924 Tennessee had passed an antievolution law, the Butler Act. Aimed at Charles Darwin's theory of evolution, the law prohibited teaching "any theory that denies the story of the Divine Creation of man as taught in the Bible."

Fundamentalists rejoiced when the Butler Act was passed, but the governor of Tennessee did not think the new law would make any difference. "Nobody believes it is going to be an active statute," he said. The American Civil Liberties Union (ACLU) disagreed. ACLU lawyers thought the act should be struck down by the courts, and they offered to pay for the defense of any teacher who wanted to "test" the law.

John Scopes, a 24-year-old high school science teacher in Dayton, Tennessee, volunteered to teach the theory of evolution to his class. As expected, Scopes was arrested and brought to trial. But his trial turned into a national showdown between fundamentalists— people who believed in a literal reading of the Bible—and modern science, between rural traditions and values and the new urban worldliness of the 1920s. Essentially the courtroom became a battleground over the place of religion in modern society.

The ACLU hired Clarence Darrow, a well-known liberal defender of unpopular causes, to take Scopes's side. The fundamentalists asked William Jennings Bryan, a three-time candidate for president and a hero to rural Americans, to take charge of the prosecution.

The trial itself occurred in a carnival atmosphere. Crowds of fundamentalists and a throng of reporters descended on Dayton in the July heat. Fundamentalists set up revival camps and offered salvation to any and all. Vendors sold hot dogs, popcorn, Bibles, and copies of Darwin's *On the Origin of Species.* In the courtroom, Bryan won the battle. The jury found Scopes guilty, although it merely fined him. Darrow, however, won the war. In the course of the trial, Darrow called Bryan to the stand.

In a lengthy cross-examination, Bryan steadfastly defended fundamentalist beliefs. Finally, Darrow asked Bryan if God had created the world in six days. Bryan responded, "Not six days of twenty-four hours"—a clear suggestion that he did not believe completely in the literal interpretation of the Bible.

Later, Scopes's fine was overturned on a technicality by an appeals court. The court also ordered the prosecutor not to seek a new trial. The Butler Act remained on the books, but it was never again enforced. Antievolution bills were introduced in 12 other states but passed in only four. More than anything else, the Scopes trial reflected the anguish of many rural Americans who saw a way of life vanishing under the onslaught of change. These rural Americans tried to preserve the values and traditions on which that way of life was based. In the end it was not so much a battle between religion and science as it was a clash between rural and urban ways of life.

> *"The very thing that made us stands in the way of our development as a civilized people.... The machine [has caused] the herding of men into towns and cities, the age of the factory.... Men all began to dress alike, eat the same foods, read the same kind of newspapers and books. Minds began to be standardized as were the clothes men wore."*
>
> —Sherwood Anderson, on America's 150th birthday, 1926

▼ Opposing attorneys Clarence Darrow (left) and William Jennings Bryan pause during the historic "Monkey Trial" in Dayton, Tennessee.

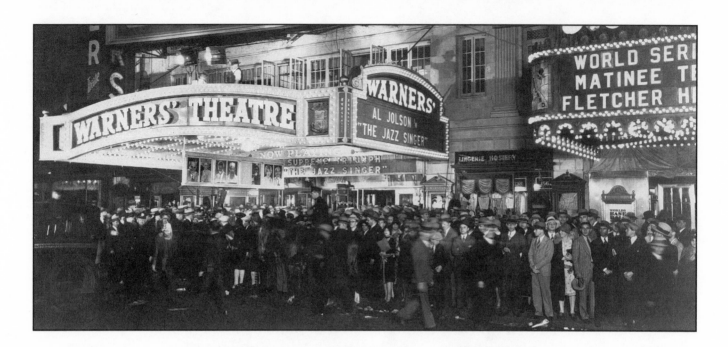

ARTS AND ENTERTAINMENT

In the arts the 1920s was a time of contrast and contradiction. Much of the decade's character was related to what had come directly before: World War I. Disillusioned by its horror—and by the materialism that followed it in the United States—young artists were part of what Gertrude Stein labeled the "lost generation." Many, including the writers Ernest Hemingway and F. Scott Fitzgerald, translated their disaffection into powerful artistic expressions. Ironically, much of this work was wildly popular, embraced by the society whose values the artists were rejecting.

The art forms of the long-underappreciated African-American culture also earned new prominence and influence in the 1920s. The most popular was jazz, a type of music that sprang directly from the rich musical traditions of black culture.

Black artists and writers also achieved a new prominence during this era, with varied works that powerfully reflected the richness of their culture.

Not everything was new, of course. Many Americans preferred their art and entertainment in more traditional forms. What was changing for them, however, was how they received it. Radio, particularly, changed the nature of entertainment in the 1920s, bringing music, sports, comedy, and news directly into homes for the first time. And the movies, still a relatively recent development, were changed forever in 1927 with the addition of sound.

In both the arts and entertainment, the only constant seemed to be change.

AT A GLANCE

▶ The Jazz Age

▶ The Harlem Renaissance

▶ The Writer's Art

▶ A Lively Era on Stage

▶ The Movies Learn to Speak

▶ Entertainment Enters America's Living Rooms

▶ New Styles in Art and Architecture

DATAFILE

Attendance and sales	1919	1929
Movie attendance (weekly)	40 mil. (1922)	80 mil.
Reading material sales (excluding educational)	$204.0 mil.	$847.0 mil.
Home audio/visual expenditures	$667.0 mil.	$713.0 mil.

The press	1919	1929
Number of daily newspapers	2,042 (1920)	1,944
Circulation	27.8 mil. (1920)	39.4 mil.
Number of magazines	4,796	5,157
Circulation	NA	202.0 mil.

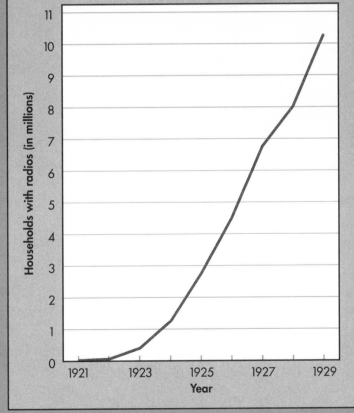

THE BIRTH OF BROADCASTING
The Number of Households with Radios, 1921–1929

Source: National Broadcasting Company.

THE JAZZ AGE

To some fundamentalist preachers, the music of the 1920s was a combination of nervousness, lawlessness, and lust. They claimed that it would destroy the nation's morals. The music of that decade, however, reflected the nation's mixture of people and cultures. Musicians of the 1920s developed a form of music uniquely American. That music was jazz. So completely did it reflect the times that the era is known as the Jazz Age.

Jazz's Development

When King Oliver's Creole Jazz Band broke into the opening bars of "Bugle Call Rag," anyone could tell that jazz and the 1920s were made for each other. "The joint stank of body musk, bootleg booze, excited people, platform sweat," wrote a visitor to a Chicago jazz club. "I couldn't see well but I was feeling all over, 'Why isn't everyone in the world here to hear this?'"

Jazz had its origins in music played at black funerals in New Orleans. As each funeral began, musicians accompanying the mourners played slow, mournful music. After the burial, however, the musicians played lively tunes to symbolize the soul's passage to heaven. As time passed, the music of New Orleans continued to develop in dance halls and neighborhood clubs. Ultimately, jazz became a blend of African-American work songs and West Indian rhythms, Protestant hymns and Creole melodies, country blues and European dance music.

The styles of individual performers exerted additional influence. Buddy Bolden's soaring cornet solos and Jelly Roll Morton's stomping piano rhythms helped shape "hot blues" into what we now consider jazz. After World War I, many out-of-work black musicians headed up the Mississippi to St. Louis, Kansas City, and Chicago or east to New York. Their music went with them, and white America soon discovered jazz.

King Oliver

A leading jazz band in Chicago during the early 1920s was Joe "King" Oliver's Creole Jazz Band. Everyone agreed that Oliver, a big, powerful man, deserved to be king.

Jazz Trumpeter Louis "Satchmo" Armstrong

▲ The young Louis Armstrong (center, holding cornet) is pictured here with King Oliver's Creole Jazz Band in Chicago, around 1922.

Louis Armstrong was born in New Orleans on Independence Day, 1900, a significant date for a new life that would help give birth to jazz—a uniquely American form of music. Even in his childhood, whenever he picked up a cornet everyone listened. Kid Ory, with whose band Armstrong often performed, reported: "Everyone in the park went wild over this boy in knee trousers who could play so great."

Armstrong made his name in the Storyville district of New Orleans. There he convinced King Oliver to be his teacher. "There's the man that's responsible for my everything in the world of Swing—Jazz—Hot—Ragtime," Armstrong said of King Oliver, one of the great cornetists of the day.

In 1918 Oliver took his band north to Chicago. Four years later, he was king of Chicago jazz, too, and he invited Armstrong to join him. Soon the student, with his great soaring solos and magnificent tone, was overshadowing his teacher.

When the Creole Jazz Band broke up over money disputes, Armstrong formed his own band, first called the Hot Five, then the Hot Seven. From 1925 to 1928, Armstrong (now playing a trumpet) and his band made a number of records that still remain among the most influential jazz recordings of all time. While Armstrong, ever the entertainer, called himself "Reverend Satchelmouth," his millions of fans around the world just called him "Satchmo."

Armstrong died in 1971, but even today many people still remember his raspy baritone voice, the trademark white handkerchief he wrapped around one hand, and his remarkable solos.

When the cornetist was about to blow a really hot tune, he hollered, "Now you'll get a chance to see Papa Joe's red underwear." He blew hard, his shirt buttons popped, and his red undershirt came shining through.

In 1923 King Oliver and his band made the first recording by a major black jazz band. A young cornet player by the name of Louis Armstrong was also featured on the record. Before long, Armstrong's breathtaking range, supple tones, and musical imagination made him a favorite with audiences in America and Europe. Many critics consider Armstrong the greatest jazz musician of all time.

The Spread of Jazz

Many great jazz musicians were women. Blues singers like Ma Rainey and Bessie Smith translated the soulful sounds of Southern blues into raw, poetic jazz songs. Lillian Hardin, a jazz pianist who later married Louis Armstrong, was one of the first women to achieve stardom as a jazz instrumentalist.

Talented white musicians also learned to play jazz. The Original Dixieland Jazz Band became an overnight sensation in New York. Chicago was a showcase for the New Orleans Rhythm Kings and the Wolverines, which featured the flowing cornet of Bix Beiderbecke.

As jazz became popular, its emphasis shifted from group improvisation to solo performance and from small combos to big bands. Musicians such as Louis Armstrong, Edward "Duke" Ellington, and Fletcher Henderson formed popular dance bands. These bands were favorites, especially in the Prohibition nightclubs and speakeasies that served mainly white audiences.

George Gershwin

A popular and talented composer of show tunes, George Gershwin wrote a "jazz concerto," a piece for piano titled *Rhapsody in Blue*. Performed in 1924 with a 23-piece jazz band, it was the musical event of the decade.

Before the concert, one musician reported, "Men and women were fighting to get in the door, pulling and mauling each other as they sometimes do at a baseball game, or a prizefight, or in the subway." While Gershwin's stunning concerto more than lived up to the crowd's expectations, their behavior showed how well jazz caught the tempo, excitement, nervousness, and frantic drive of the 1920s.

Culture

THE HARLEM RENAISSANCE

Harlem was a hot spot of the 1920s. When the hit musical *Shuffle Along* played to packed audiences on Broadway in 1921, many people discovered black music and dancing. Now the sounds of jazz poured out of more than 500 night spots in Harlem alone.

White people flocked to the Cotton Club and Connie's Inn to dance the Charleston to the big band jazz of Duke Ellington and Fletcher

THE BLUES

The style of music known as the blues evolved from the work songs of black slaves. Both in melody and lyric, the blues reflect the hard times and suffering of African-Americans.

The blues became popular after W. C. Handy began to adapt black folk songs to a new style of popular music. Handy, known as the "Father of the Blues," published "Memphis Blues" in 1912 and "St. Louis Blues" in 1914.

Gertrude "Ma" Rainey became one of the first singers to perform the blues when she traveled with black troupes in the early 1900s. Known as the "Mother of Blues," she made several records for Paramount.

That same year, Bessie Smith's career took off. Smith, who had been discovered by Rainey, became known as the "Empress of the Blues." From 1923 to 1930, she made as many as 200 recordings, some of which sold more than 100,000 copies a week.

HIT PARADE, 1919–1929

1919 "A Pretty Girl Is Like a Melody"
1920 "I'll Be with You in Apple Blossom Time"
1921 "Second Hand Rose"
1922 "Georgia"
1923 "Yes! We Have No Bananas"
1924 "California, Here I Come"
1925 "If You Knew Suzy"
1926 "Bye Bye Blackbird"
1927 "I'm Looking over a Four-Leaf Clover"
1928 "You're the Cream in My Coffee"
1929 "Singin' in the Rain"

Henderson. The swarming crowds "found Harlem exotic and colorful," as one observer put it. "To them it seemed a citadel of jazz and laughter where gaiety began after midnight."

Amid the sounds of jazz and the blues, African-Americans discovered a respect for their own culture. They spoke with pride of their own identity and lashed out against the racist attitudes of many white people.

Black writers who moved to Harlem from the South took up these themes. They expressed the spirit of the so-called New Negro, who had returned from World War I with a new sense of dignity. This explosion of black pride and culture found similar expression in black communities across America. The movement became known, however, as the Harlem Renaissance, for the community where the rebirth was most visible and influential.

A New Spirit

Alain Locke, a graduate of Harvard University and a professor of literature at Howard University, was one of the important leaders of the Harlem Renaissance. In his collection *The New Negro,* Locke brought together the work of black writers and artists who were exploring their culture in poems, stories, essays, plays, and art. The new generation of African-Americans is "vibrant with a new psychology," Locke wrote; "the new spirit is awake in the masses."

Locke followed up a theme that W. E. B. Du Bois had sounded in his 1903 book *The Souls of Black Folk.* With elegance and passion, Du Bois argued that black people could achieve equality with white people by developing pride in their own heritage. Only then, Du Bois claimed, could black people be truly liberated.

Continuing the Challenge

Many black writers and artists of the 1920s took Du Bois's words to heart. Zora Neale Hurston, an anthropologist, wrote plays and short stories featuring the black folktales she heard as a child. The poet Countee Cullen, the artist Aaron Douglas, the actor and singer Paul Robeson—all joined in the celebration of black culture. Together, they proclaimed that blacks would no longer accept second-class status in American life.

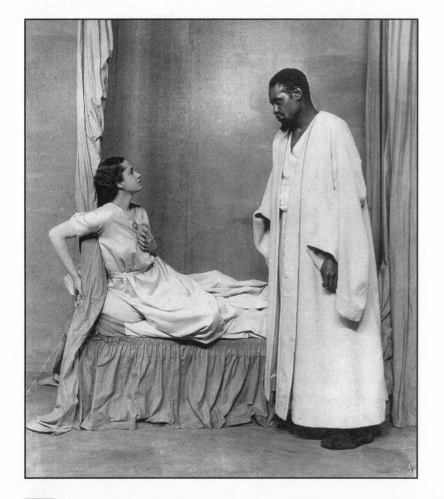

▼ The actor and singer Paul Robeson was one of the African-American artists gaining attention during the 1920s. Here he plays the title role in Shakespeare's *Othello* opposite British actress Peggy Ashcroft as Desdemona.

Jamaican-born Claude McKay, who settled in Harlem, challenged black people to fight for equality in his poems "If We Must Die" and "The White City." In his 1927 autobiography *Home to Harlem,* McKay probed to the heart of the matter. He was fascinated with the rich and varied skin tones of people who call themselves black. Chocolate, chestnut, coffee, ebony, cream, yellow—all black, and all proud, alive with a new spirit of freedom and equality.

Literature

THE WRITER'S ART

Another brash new generation of American writers burst on the scene in the 1920s, bringing energy and imagination to the written word. Many also brought a growing conviction that something was terribly wrong with the nation's self-centered, small-town attitudes and its money-centered, big-business values.

Langston Hughes: Voice of Harlem

Langston Hughes, a gifted black poet who was born in Joplin, Missouri, in 1902, became a leading voice in the Harlem Renaissance. His "discovery" as a poet is the stuff of legend. While working as a busboy in a Washington, D.C., hotel, Hughes recognized one of the diners as the poet Vachel Lindsay. Hughes rushed up to Lindsay's table, placed several poems by the poet's plate, then fled. When Hughes picked up a newspaper the next morning, he discovered that Lindsay had told the world about his poems. Within a year, the publisher Alfred Knopf brought out the first volume of Hughes's poetry, *The Weary Blues.* The book was widely acclaimed.

Part of Hughes's genius lay in his ability to blend jazz themes and rhythms with comic and tragic elements in his realistic portrayal of black life. He celebrated the culture of black people, even the poorest ones.

In one of his essays, Hughes explained: "If white people are pleased, we are glad. If they are not, it doesn't matter. We know we are beautiful. And ugly too. The tom tom cries, and the tom tom laughs."

Hughes's most enduring gift to literature may be his belief that all people shared a common life, in suffering if not in gladness. Hughes's poem "Afraid" illustrated this belief as well as his dramatic skill.

> We cry among the
>   skyscrapers
> As our ancestors
> Cried among the palms in
>   Africa
> Because we are alone,
> It is night,
> And we're afraid.

► F. Scott Fitzgerald is shown at near right with his wife, Zelda, also a writer, in 1920. At far right is H. L. Mencken, the "man who hates everything," and the editor of the influential magazine *American Mercury*.

Cynical Novels

In 1920 F. Scott Fitzgerald published his first novel, *This Side of Paradise*. The book served as a bible for rebellious, college-age "flaming youth." In 1925 he published *The Great Gatsby*, considered by many as the classic reflection of the materialistic values and decadence of the 1920s.

Sinclair Lewis, in his best-selling book *Main Street* (1920), took a cynical look at life in America's small towns through the eyes of Carol, the book's city-bred heroine:

> Main Street with its two-story brick shops, its story-and-a-half wooden residences, its muddy expanse from concrete walk to walk, its huddle of Fords and lumber wagons, was too small to absorb her. The broad, straight, unenticing gashes of the streets let in the grasping prairie on every side. She realized the vastness and the emptiness of the land.

Lewis's 1922 novel *Babbitt* focused on its title character, a typical, narrow-minded businessman of the 1920s—a type commonly referred to subsequently as a "Babbitt." For his work, Lewis became in 1930 the first American to win the Nobel Prize in literature.

H. L. Mencken may have been the most entertaining of the social critics. Through his very popular

Selected Best-Sellers, 1919–1929

Year	Title	Author
1919	The Four Horsemen of the Apocalypse	V. Blasco Ibañez
1920	The Man of the Forest	Zane Grey
1921	Main Street	Sinclair Lewis
1922	If Winter Comes	A. S. M. Hutchinson
1923	Black Oxen	Gertrude Atherton
1924	So Big	Edna Ferber
1925	Surroundings	A. Hamilton Gibbs
1926	The Private Life of Helen of Troy	John Erskine
1927	Elmer Gantry	Sinclair Lewis
1928	The Bridge of San Luis Rey	Thornton Wilder
1929	All Quiet on the Western Front	Erich Maria Remarque

newspaper columns and magazine articles, "the man who hates everything" aimed his barbs at everyone. Do-gooders, he once quipped, are motivated by "the haunting fear that someone, somewhere, might be happy." "What we need," he declared, "is more sin."

Other writers added their distinctive voices to the written art of the decade. Edith Wharton wrote a book a year, often giving a woman's view of upper-class life. In *The Age of Innocence* (1920), for which she received a Pulitzer Prize, Wharton described the conflicts that arise when money and moral values clash. Kathleen Norris published *Certain People of Importance* (1922) and became one of the most popular and highly paid women writers. William Faulkner explored Southern life in powerful books like *The Marble Faun*, a book of poetry published in 1924, and *The Sound and the Fury*, a novel written in 1929.

Stimulating Poetry

Poets were also very popular. One was e.e. cummings, who showed a playful and imaginative use of words and punctuation. In 1925 Ezra Pound published the first sections of the *Cantos*, an attempt to

American Literature and the Lost Generation

Following the horror of World War I, some writers and artists felt out of place in the big-business atmosphere America had developed. They believed the United States was "the enemy of the artist, of the man who cannot produce something tangible when the five o'clock whistle blows." A few decided to move to Europe, especially Paris, where living costs were lower and a sizable community of artists resided.

When the 1920s began, Gertrude Stein and Ernest Hemingway were already living in Paris. Stein went to Paris in 1903, where she wrote plays, operas, and books, all of them using language in bold new ways. Stein also encouraged many Americans living in Paris—Hemingway among them—in their literary careers. It was Stein who called Hemingway and his friends the "lost generation."

▼ ▼ ▼

"Here was a new generation, ... dedicated more than the last to the fear of poverty and the worship of success; grown up to find all gods dead, all wars fought, all faiths in man shaken."

—F. Scott Fitzgerald,
This Side of Paradise, 1920

Along with F. Scott Fitzgerald, it was Hemingway, however, who best captured the spirit of the lost generation. His writing style was compact and direct, simple and sparse. It fit in well with the stoic courage of his heroes and heroines. He wrote his first major novel, *The Sun Also Rises*, in Paris. Stein's "lost generation" quote was on its title page. When the book was published in 1926, Hemingway became an instant literary star at the age of 27.

The book told the story of a mostly drunken, desperately carefree band of Americans who traveled from Paris to Spain. They drank a lot and quarreled even more, risked their lives in the annual running of the bulls in Pamplona, Spain, and fell in and out of love with one another—anything to escape the empty despair of everyday life. Like Hemingway himself, his characters—and the group of Americans they embodied—groped in vain for something of merit to believe in.

recount the story of civilization, a work Pound continued to write throughout his life. T. S. Eliot became famous with the influential *Waste Land* (1922).

Edna St. Vincent Millay wrote poems of sentiment and wit. Robert Frost penned haunting poetic portraits of New England. Edgar A. Guest charmed readers with sentimental Midwestern ballads. No work, however, captures the contradictions of the 1920s better than Millay's poem "First Fig":

My candle burns at both ends;
It will not last the night;
But, ah, my foes, and, oh, my friends—
It gives a lovely light.

The 1920s was an extraordinary decade of brilliant writing, and the influence of its writers remains strong even today.

Major Literary Figures, 1919–1929

Author	Major Work	Year
Sherwood Anderson	Dark Laughter	1925
Willa Cather	My Mortal Enemy	1926
William Faulkner	The Sound and the Fury	1929
F. Scott Fitzgerald	The Great Gatsby	1925
Ernest Hemingway	The Sun Also Rises	1926
James Joyce	Ulysses	1922
Sinclair Lewis	Arrowsmith	1925
H. L. Mencken	The American Language	1919
Edith Wharton	The Age of Innocence	1920

Poet	Major Work	Year
e. e. cummings	Tulips and Chimneys	1923
T. S. Eliot	The Waste Land	1922
Robert Frost	New Hampshire	1923
Langston Hughes	The Weary Blues	1926
Edna St. Vincent Millay	The Buck in the Snow	1928
Ezra Pound	Umbra	1920
William Butler Yeats	The Tower	1928

The Popular Press

During the 1920s, magazines and newspapers increased circulation. More people had learned to read, more people had leisure time for reading, and more people had money to buy the magazines and newspapers of the popular press.

The *Saturday Evening Post, National Geographic,* and other established magazines reached new peaks in circulation, while dozens of new publications appeared. *Vogue* defined fashion trends for the nation's elite. Among sophisticated audiences, H. L. Mencken's *American Mercury* may have been the most influential magazine of the era. *Time,* the *New Yorker, Life, Harper's Bazaar,* and *Reader's Digest* sought to inform, entertain, and amuse their readers in their distinctive ways.

True Story magazine had another agenda. Its 2 million readers feasted on stories like "The Primitive Lover" and "What I Told My Daughter the Night Before Her Marriage."

A host of **tabloid** newspapers, led by New York's *Daily News,* used racy writing, lavish illustrations, and lurid headlines to thrill readers with sensational stories, most often about crime and romance-gone-wrong. ROASTED ALIVE, read one tabloid headline about an execution at a prison.

"My dream of love has turned into a hideous, revolting nightmare," began another story, headlined WHY I LEFT DADDY BROWNING. Many feared tabloid journalism would destroy people's minds, but millions of Americans read the tabloids anyway, even if they never admitted it.

Homespun Humorist Will Rogers

Will Rogers, a small-town boy from Oklahoma, grew up to be a cowboy, then became a rope expert in a Wild West show. Audiences laughed as much at his jokes, however, as they admired his skill with a lariat. Rogers eventually began writing a newspaper column about politics and American life that was always fair and usually funny. An estimated 40 million people read his homespun humor and folksy observations each week in more than 350 newspapers nationwide. Here are a few examples from America's "poet lariat," as he used to call himself.

▸ "With Congress, every time they make a joke it's a law; every time they make a law it's a joke."

▸ "Everyone is ignorant, only on different subjects."

▸ "All I know is just what I read in the papers."

▸ "What the country needs is dirtier fingernails and cleaner minds."

▸ "Nothing you can't spell will ever work."

▸ "In Hollywood, the woods are full of people that learned to write, but evidently can't read. If they could read their stuff, they'd stop writing."

▸ "The income tax has made more liars out of the American people than gold has."

▸ "A holding company is a thing where you hand an accomplice the goods while the policeman searches you."

Theater

A LIVELY ERA ON STAGE

With radio bringing live entertainment into people's homes for the first time, theater in the 1920s declined in many areas. But in major cities, especially New York, people still looked to the theater for light-hearted musical reviews and sentimental comedies.

Mass Entertainment

One favorite Broadway show was *Abie's Irish Rose*, a tear-jerking romance between a Jewish boy and an Irish girl. When the play opened in 1922, one critic wrote: "'The Rotters' is no longer the worst play in town!" *Abie's Irish Rose* is "something awful, among the season's worst." People said they were embarrassed to see the play, but they did anyway. It ran for 2,327 performances over a period of almost five and a half years, setting a record for length of run up to that time.

For people in the 1920s entertainment was an escape from their everyday routine. Musical reviews were an immensely popular way of losing themselves in the magic of the theatrical moments.

The dancers Fred and Adele Astaire dazzled audiences in *Stop Flirting*. George Gershwin, the king of show tunes, captivated theatergoers with *Lady Be Good!* and *Funny Face*. The Ziegfeld *Follies*,

MAGAZINE SURVIVORS

Three of today's most popular magazines were born during the 1920s. *Reader's Digest,* the monthly collection of condensed articles gathered from other publications, was founded in 1921 by DeWitt and Lila Wallace. *Time,* a newsweekly, was created by Briton Hadden and Henry Luce in 1923. The *New Yorker,* a weekly literary and arts-related magazine, was founded by Harold Ross in 1925.

▼ Eugene O'Neill's psychological dramas were among the more noteworthy serious plays of the era. O'Neill is generally regarded as one of the finest playwrights in American history.

an enormously successful series of yearly music and comedy reviews, brought black jazz musicians, blues singers, and dancers into the mainstream of American theater.

It was *Show Boat,* however, that marked the birth of the modern American musical. Written by Jerome Kern and Oscar Hammerstein II and based on a novel by Edna Ferber, it opened on December 27, 1927.

Show Boat discarded the conventional structure of a musical review. Instead, in the manner of an opera, it combined a serious plot about life on the Mississippi River with complementary music. Its success made it the model for the modern musical.

Serious Drama
Perhaps the most powerful voice in serious American drama during the 1920s was that of Eugene O'Neill. He wrote more than 20 plays during the decade, including *Anna Christie* and *The Emperor Jones.* O'Neill won Pulitzer Prizes for three of his plays, and gained for American drama its first serious attention abroad.

O'Neill's plays were somber, dwelling on dark themes of insanity, murder, suicide, and death. "To me, the tragic alone has that significant beauty which is truth," he once wrote in a newspaper article. "It is the meaning of life—and the hope. The noblest is eternally the most tragic. . . . Damn the optimists anyway! They make life so darned hopeless!"

The Birth of Modern Dance
The influence of the American dancer Isadora Duncan continued to expand during the 1920s. Duncan was a free spirit who expressed herself through her dancing. In doing so, she rejected the rigid movements and conventions of ballet and virtually invented what has since become known as "modern dance."

Duncan's personal life was as dramatic as her dancing. It included the accidental drowning of her two children and a brief, disastrous marriage to a Russian poet. She died tragically in 1927 when the scarf she was wearing became entangled in the wheels of an automobile in which she was riding.

Martha Graham was one of the young American dancers influenced by Duncan. Graham's distinctive style of dance emphasized angular movements and thrusts from the center of the dancer's body. Her new style of dance was introduced to the public in a 1926 recital that astonished and outraged its audience.

Graham went on to become one of the most important figures in the history of modern dance, both as a performer and as a choreographer. Her career was to span seven decades.

Religion as Theater: Evangelists Sunday and McPherson

The majority of Americans in the 1920s practiced their religion of choice in the traditional way by going to weekly church services where ministers and priests performed their rituals, preached their sermons, and passed the collection plates. Some Americans, however, took to a more flamboyant type of preacher and preaching that employed aspects of show business.

One was Billy Sunday (above). A former professional baseball player, Sunday underwent a conversion experience in 1886 and subsequently became a Presby-terian minister. As a traveling evangelist, he used old-fashioned emotions and hell-fire and brimstone techniques to draw huge crowds to his revival camps. At one point, the number of his followers was estimated at 1 million. With his gymnastic preaching and his colorful language, he raked in huge profits until about 1920, when his popularity began to wane.

Evangelist Aimee Semple McPherson (below right), on the other hand, took the love-and-sunshine approach and never mentioned hell in her International Church of Foursquare Gospel. The daughter of a missionary and traveling preacher, McPherson came into her own in 1921, when she spoke at an outdoor rally in San Diego and became known as a faith healer.

With her newfound success, McPherson built the Angelus Temple, a magnificent steel and concrete palace in Los Angeles, the entertainment capital of the world. The temple seated more than 5,000, and all the seats were filled for every service.

With a huge choir, a brass band, a pipe organ, elegant draperies, colored lights, vases of flowers, and a team of special-effects men, McPherson's services were as dramatic as some of Broadway's shows. *The Sunshine Hour* was her own radio program. It was broadcast on her own radio station, which also aired Bible readings, sermonettes, and sacred songs between services. While McPherson's services were pure theater, everyone was entertained and uplifted.

Film

THE MOVIES LEARN TO SPEAK

"Go to a movie . . . and let yourself go," encouraged an advertisement in the *Saturday Evening Post*. One movie advertisement from this decade offered audiences all the excitement they lacked in their daily lives. The ad promised scenes with "brilliant men, beautiful jazz babies, champagne baths, midnight revels."

The 1920s was a time of escape and abandon, and nowhere could more fantasy be found than at a movie theater. Some theaters were "picture palaces"—grand structures decorated with lavishly painted ceilings, plush seats, thick carpets, huge mirrors, and marble staircases. In summer, fans blew air over ice blocks to cool the moviegoers. With most Americans going to the movies at least once a week, more and more movie theaters were built in cities across the nation.

The movies of the 1920s were a powerful social force that both reflected and helped shape American values. Movies brought Americans closer together by giving them a common popular culture.

Screen Idols

Americans roared with laughter at the antics of three silent film stars at the peak of their comic powers. Few moviegoers could forget a hungry Charlie Chaplin, dressed in a tuxedo, picking at a plate of boiled shoe leather in *The Gold Rush*. Chaplin's best-known alter ego was the Little Tramp, the endearing character with baggy pants, a derby hat, oversized shoes, and an odd walk.

Everyone enjoyed the sight of Harold Lloyd dangling from the hands of a huge clock far above the street below in *Safety Last*.

Film Stardom and the Transition to Sound

▲ Swedish film actress Greta Garbo wears an orchid in this 1929 portrait.

In a silent movie, the actor was a mime, communicating with gestures and facial expressions. In a "talkie," the actor communicated, with words as well as gestures and facial expressions. Everything had to say, "This is a real person." Some stars of the silent films were unable to make the transition to the demands of sound.

During the silent era, for example, Clara Bow was "The Hottest Jazz Baby in Films." She had "It," according to Elinor Glyn, an author of a novel called *It* and other popular love stories. According to Glyn, anyone with "It" had to have "that strange magnetism which attracts both sexes."

Once everyone learned Clara Bow had "It," this tiny, boyishly built starlet with big eyes and dimpled knees became one of the top five box office attractions in Hollywood. Then came talkies, and the thick Brooklyn accent of the "It" girl destroyed her career in films.

In contrast, the talkies were as kind to Greta Garbo as they were cruel to Clara Bow. Garbo had an alluring voice that enabled her to create true-to-life characters that leaped off the screen.

Grand Hotel, Anna Karenina, Queen Christina, Camille, and *Ninotchka* were just a few of Garbo's many screen triumphs. Today people consider these films to be classics—lasting sounds and images of one of the greatest film actresses of all time.

Lloyd specialized in playing the shy, naive character called upon to perform the unexpected heroic act. *Grandma's Boy* (1922), *The Freshman* (1925), and *The Kid Brother* (1927) are among his other hits of the decade.

Moviegoers smiled at Buster Keaton (who never smiled on screen) as a prehistoric caveman taking a bath in *The Three Ages.* They cheered the gags and stunts in his many films, such as *Sherlock Junior* (1924) and *The General* (1926).

These three represented comedy at its slapstick best. They shared other qualities as well. All three participated in the writing, directing, and producing of their films. Each had also developed a distinctive style of comedy that worked without words. With rumors that new film technology incorporating sound was just around the corner, each viewed the future anxiously.

The famous comedy team of Stan Laurel and Oliver Hardy was created in 1926, when they were teamed in *Putting Pants on Philip.* The thin, timid Laurel and the fat, aggressive Hardy were a perfect fit. In their case, what opposites attracted was large audiences.

During the 1920s the public idolized movie stars, often not so much for their acting as for what they stood for on the screen. Audiences wept when Mary Pickford,

THE OSCARS

The Academy of Motion Picture Arts and Sciences was established in 1927 to present annual awards, commonly known as Oscars, in recognition of noteworthy achievements in the motion picture industry. The first Oscars were presented in 1929. *Wings* was named best movie for that year. Janet Gaynor won for best actress and Emil Jannings for best actor.

▲ "The Sheik" was a film character made famous by actor Rudolph Valentino. Valentino was beloved by millions of American women who attended movies during the 1920s.

"America's Sweetheart," was forced to fend off a villain with a pitchfork in *Sparrows*. They marveled as the exotic and hot-tempered Pola Negri danced sensuously in *Bella Donna*.

Fans flocked to the films of Greta Garbo. Her love scenes in *Flesh and the Devil* brought to the silver screen a stunning new presence, at once icy and smoldering. One of Garbo's costars said simply, "She was the greatest actress ever seen on the screen."

Other leading ladies crowded the silver screen. There was the sophisticated Gloria Swanson. Joan Crawford played the popular screen flapper. Equally glamorous were the romantic leading men of the decade. The elegant John Barrymore captivated many female hearts in *Beau Brummel*. The flamboyant Douglas Fairbanks thrilled romantics everywhere in *The Thief of Bagdad*.

Finally, in 1926, many hearts were broken by the early death of Rudolph Valentino, the most famous of the screen lovers. His best-known films were *The Sheik* and *The Son of the Sheik*. Every week, America's screen idols gave audiences another adventure to relish, another romance to dream about.

New Movie Trends

The movie industry changed rapidly during the 1920s. Cecil B. De Mille introduced movie audiences to extravagant productions of such screen epics as *The Ten Commandments*. With a cast of thousands, vast sets, and complex action scenes, De Mille expanded Hollywood's idea of what a movie could show.

Filmmaker Robert Flaherty used the movie camera to focus on the present. His realistic portrait of the life of an actual Eskimo, *Nanook of the North*, gave audiences their first glimpse at a filmed documentary.

But the most dramatic change in film came on October 6, 1927, in New York City. *The Jazz Singer*, which starred Al Jolson, ushered in a new era in movies—the talkies. Sound brought an end to the mimicry and gestures used by silent film stars.

Phonofilm had been showing in New York with a recorded musical sound track since 1923. But *The Jazz Singer* was the first feature film with a sound track containing actors' voices. Jolson's first words in the film, "You ain't heard nothin' yet," could have been the new slogan for the movie industry. By 1930 the silent films had flickered out, and the talkies were pulling 110 million Americans into movie theaters each week.

ENTERTAINMENT ENTERS AMERICA'S LIVING ROOMS

Radio brought sounds from across the nation and around the world into American homes for the first time. It enriched the lives of people on dairy farms in Iowa, in the coal mines of West Virginia, and in the factories of Detroit.

Radio gave listeners "front seats in the theater of the world." One station's programming for a week, according to an advertisement, included addresses by the president of the United States, concerts by the New York Philharmonic Orchestra, a Sunday morning church service, a blow-by-blow ringside report of a heavyweight boxing championship, music, educational talks, and last-minute news reports from all over the country.

Listening to the radio quickly became America's favorite pastime, capturing both the attention and the imagination of the nation. Radio started trends and shaped opinions, made new expressions popular, and suggested new ways of dressing and eating. Almost everyone, for example, picked up phrases from *Amos 'n' Andy*, one of the decade's most popular radio comedies: "I'se regusted!" "Holy mackerel, Andy!" "Now ain't that sumpin!"

In 1925 the popular phrase, "I'm going back to the wagon, boys. These shoes are killin' me," was picked up by many listeners of the *Grand Ole Opry*. Listeners across the nation discussed with their neighbors the ups and downs of life on *Real Folks*, a radio drama.

▲ Listening to radio programs became a popular activity for American families during the 1920s.

The first radio broadcast was a news program. News and public service broadcasts continued to attract listeners. In 1921 President Harding delivered his Armistice Day address live from the Tomb of the Unknown Soldier at Arlington National Cemetery. The following year, he broadcast the first presidential news conference. News readers like Graham McNamee gained wide popularity for their unique way of blending news and editorial comment.

Radio was the first medium to bring people news as it happened. Radio listeners on May 21, 1927, were thrilled when Lowell Thomas reported the news from Paris: "Charles A. Lindbergh . . . landed at Le Bourget Airport, Paris, at 5:24 this afternoon, thus becoming the first person to fly from New York to Paris nonstop." Farm news and stock market reports were closely followed by listeners whose primary interest during the 1920s was making money.

CHANGING VALUES

The most popular radio program of all time was *Amos 'n' Andy*. First broadcast in 1926, it featured two white Chicago actors playing a black cabdriver (Andy) and his friend (Amos), who worked at the Fresh-Air Taxi Company. By 1929 the show ran five nights a week. Rather than try to compete, movie theaters across the nation stopped showing movies during its broadcast time and played the radio program instead. The program later fell out of favor, faulted by blacks and whites alike for perpetuating a stereotypical view of black people.

▼ Georgia O'Keeffe's 1926 painting of a calla lily exemplifies her original and distinctive style.

Music also attracted a huge radio audience. Vincent Lopez, radio's first band leader, began his 1921 broadcast from the Hotel Taft in New York City with "Lopez speaking. . . ." The New York Philharmonic and Philadelphia orchestras, jazz by Paul Whiteman and Duke Ellington, the "hotcha" rhythm of the Cliquot Club Eskimos, the crooning of Rudy Vallee—these entertainers and many more filled American homes with music throughout the decade.

In addition to drama, news, and music, radio offered baseball games and other sporting events, weather reports, talks on baby care and auto repair, programs for morning exercise, and evening prayers. In large cities, some stations broadcast programs in foreign languages for the major immigrant groups. Radio had indeed become much more than a household utility. It gave everyone an ear to the world.

Many rural Americans were especially grateful for the benefits of radio. With the flip of a switch they could dispel their isolation with information and music. For them radio offered a convenient connection with the outside world.

Visual Arts

NEW STYLES IN ART AND ARCHITECTURE

The artists of the 1920s portrayed America as a nation roaring with pleasure. They also looked beyond pleasure seeking to reveal hidden truths in the ordinary and not-so-ordinary lives of other Americans.

Varied Art

The quiet virtues of small-town America were displayed in Grant Wood's *Dinner for Threshers,* which depicts an Iowa harvesting crew gathered at a table, eating their noonday meal. The sunshine and blue sky added radiance to the farmyard scene shown in *Baptism in Kansas* by John Steuart Curry. One of John Sloan's etchings captured two ladies gaily chatting on a park bench in New York's Washington Square.

In a different light, Reginald Marsh's etching of *Julius's Annex* gave a glimpse of furtive, backroom dealings in a seedy New York speakeasy. Wood Gaylor revealed both the opulence and the decadence of urban life in *Bob's Party Number One*.

Like Marsh, Georgia O'Keeffe focused on the American city as a wilderness of machines and concrete. The jackhammer workers and derrick loaders in Marsh's sketches seem overwhelmed by the machines they operated. O'Keeffe's paintings of a stark, smog-choked New York City created a strong sense of loneliness and foreboding.

During the late 1920s, O'Keeffe began work on a series of paintings of flowers, for which she became well known. These colorful closeups were almost magical in their impact. In 1929 she spent a summer in New Mexico. There she became inspired by the desert landscape and the light, both of which would influence her paintings in terms of subject and style.

Form and Function

The architects of the period were also influenced by the machines and industry of the 1920s. This could be seen most dramatically in the work and teaching of the German architect Walter Gropius. In 1919 Gropius founded the Bauhaus, a school of design in Weimar, Germany. There he introduced the principles of architecture and design upon which the movement called "modernism" is based.

The Bauhaus style was one of reducing design to its essential elements—"less is more," in the words of Ludwig Mies van der Rohe, one

▲ The rooms of the New Hotel Jefferson in St. Louis are an example of art deco design. Popular in the 1920s and 1930s, art deco featured geometric shapes, streamlined forms, and industrial materials, such as chrome, plastic, and aluminum.

of Gropius's students. Based on the notion that form follows function, the modernist designs emphasized their own structures and materials. The buildings tended to be simple, spare, and geometric, typically constructed of steel, concrete, and glass.

While modernism would soon become the dominating influence in architecture in the United States, most American architects of the 1920s had not yet turned away from decoration. But like the influential American architect Frank Lloyd Wright, they had embraced the new materials and technology and were using them to express themselves in new ways.

One example of this trend was the style known as Art Deco, which became popular in the 1920s. Art deco design was sleek and sophisticated, emphasizing geometric patterns and modern, streamlined forms. Famous buildings of the era that exhibit the influence of art deco include New York City's Chrysler Building and Radio City Music Hall.

SPORTS AND LEISURE

With leisure increasing during the 1920s, Americans devoted more time and enthusiasm to sports. They hit, threw, swung at, and rolled more balls than ever before. The number of golf courses in the country, for example, jumped from fewer than 2,000 in 1920 to more than 6,000 in 1930. The number of bowling teams grew from 5,000 to more than 40,000 during the period.

Even more Americans, however, enjoyed being spectators at sporting events. Millions flocked to baseball, football, and basketball games. They attended boxing, wrestling, and tennis matches. They lost and won money at horse races. The 1920s spread a lavish banquet for the nation's sports fans. For those who could not attend sporting events in person, radio allowed them to follow their favorite teams and heroes in a new way.

AT A GLANCE

- ▶ The Golden Age of Sportswriting
- ▶ Baseball Comes Back from the Brink
- ▶ College Football's Greatest Legends
- ▶ The Dempsey-Tunney Era
- ▶ Tilden and Wills Make Tennis Big
- ▶ The Legendary Bobby Jones
- ▶ The Champion and the Channel Swimmer

In the 1920s the world of sports was dominated by a few individual and team stars. These sports giants became legends in their own time, competing with business people and movie stars as the idols of the decade. Babe Ruth, Bill Tilden, Red Grange, Johnny Weismuller, Bobby Jones—even today their names conjure their athletic magic.

In one prominent case, the hero was a coach. Knute Rockne (above, center) led his Notre Dame teams to remarkable records and brought new popularity to college football.

The energy and zaniness of the 1920s found an outlet in its fashions and fads. The flappers with their rising hemlines and the flagpole sitters with their crazy contests thumbed their noses at the nation's traditional conservative habits.

DATAFILE

Sports

World records as of 1925	Men	Women
Track and field		
100-yd. dash	9.5″	11.0″
Mile	4′10.4″	NA
High jump	6.7 ft.	5.0 ft.
Swimming		
100-m. freestyle	57.4″	1′12.2″

Leisure

	1919	1929
Average workweek	46.3 hrs.	44.2 hrs.
Attendance		
Baseball (major leagues)	6.8 mil.	9.8 mil.
National parks	757,000	2.8 mil.
Bicycle sales	470,000	310,000

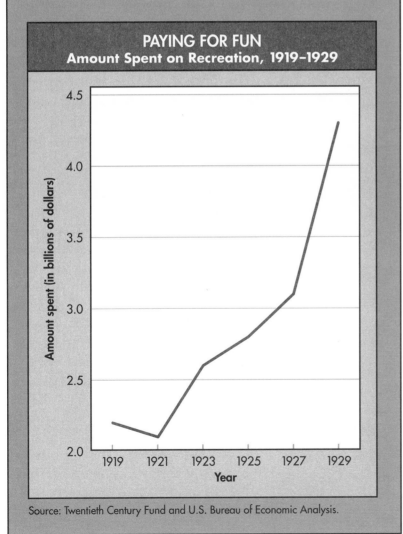

PAYING FOR FUN
Amount Spent on Recreation, 1919–1929

Source: Twentieth Century Fund and U.S. Bureau of Economic Analysis.

Sports Journalism

THE GOLDEN AGE OF SPORTSWRITING

The 1920s, quipped one observer, was the decade when Americans began to read the front page of their newspapers only after reading the sports section. There they found stirring accounts of the latest accomplishments in sports. Most Americans during the decade cared less about German war reparations or the fate of the League of Nations than about Ty Cobb's batting average, Jack Dempsey's workout schedule, or Bill Tilden's latest victories on the tennis court.

Sports stories were real news stories, and people turned to them first. The craze for sports was reflected in sports journalism and in the casual, sporty styles of dress that characterized the era.

As the nation's interest in sports skyrocketed, sportswriters and commentators became major figures both in the sports world and on the literary scene. Some sportswriting during the period was hopelessly melodramatic, but much of it was colorful, inventive, and entertaining. Grantland Rice, Paul Gallico, John Kiernan, Damon Runyon, Ring Lardner, and Westbrook Pegler were among the best of this new generation of sports journalists. Even "serious" writers like H. L. Mencken and George Bernard Shaw chronicled the triumphs of baseball's Babe Ruth and the exploits of football's Red Grange. The major sports figures of the 1920s earned fame through their talents, but their legends were secured by journalists.

By the 1920s skirts were becoming shorter, and women were showing off their legs—unless, of course, they lived in Utah.

In 1921 Utah legislators proposed a bill that called for the imprisonment of any woman who wore her skirt higher than 3 inches above her ankles.

What reader, after all, could resist Kiernan's jingle:

> My voice may be loud above the
>   crowd
> And my words just a bit uncouth,
> But I'll stand and shout till the last
>   man's out:
> "There was never a guy like Ruth!"

Fashion

SPORTS' GROWING INFLUENCE

The fashion trends of the 1920s reflected the interest in sports as well as the affluence and abandon of the postwar era. Women in the 1920s sought freedom from traditional values and escape from the dowdy "Gibson Girl" style of earlier years. Designers introduced daring new styles and promoted them in advertisements and the movies.

► Many women in the 1920s rejected traditional feminine clothing of the past in favor of the new styles of the "flapper."

The characteristic woman of the 1920s was a "flapper" who took on a carefree, boyish look. She raised her hemline to scandalous new heights, bobbed her hair, wrapped her chest to make it flat, and rolled down her flesh-colored silk stockings. Slim, drop-waisted dresses became the rage, as did fur coats and bell-shaped hats called cloches.

Flappers accented their new look with a bold application of makeup. The popular emphasis on clothing with a sporty, casual style created a decade-long boom for the fashion industry.

Men's fashions were often just as trendy. "Patent-leather hair," slicked back and parted in the center, gave young men the look of the decade's most famous screen lover, Rudolph Valentino. For trousers, the fashion-conscious man chose roomy "oxford bags." Saddle shoes and a loose-fitting sweater often completed the look.

Fads, Games, and Leisure Pursuits

The *Saturday Evening Post* accurately summed up the 1920s when it wrote that Americans were "first in war, first in peace, first in tree-sitting, gum chewing, peanut pushing and bobbing up and down in water." Americans found many new ways to amuse themselves. In 1921 in Atlantic City, New Jersey, promoters held the first Miss America contest in a scheme to make money and promote the city. Crossword puzzles, first published in book form by Simon and Schuster, provided many people with pleasant diversions from everyday life.

The 1920s also became famous for the staggering number of fads that swept the nation. Contract bridge and the ancient Chinese game of mah-jongg became the parlor games of choice for the up-to-date crowd. Pie-eating contests, dance marathons, rocking-chair derbies, and cross-country races were also popular. People who could talk the fastest, eat the most, or dance the longest won instant, if fleeting, fame.

Symbolizing the special zaniness of the 1920s was "Shipwreck" Kelly. He reached fame for his flag-pole-sitting record of 559 hours, a little more than 23 full days.

BASEBALL COMES BACK FROM THE BRINK

The year was 1919, and major-league baseball was in trouble. The year before the Cincinnati Reds had defeated the Chicago White Sox in the World Series. Then it was discovered that gamblers had paid eight White Sox players to lose the Series. Although these players were eventually banned from baseball, the integrity of major-league baseball had been put at risk.

A Game at Risk

Some said the "Black Sox" scandal, as it became known, was a unique blemish on an otherwise honorable game, but facts suggest otherwise. One baseball historian claims "the Black Sox scandal was merely the largest and ugliest wart of a disease that had infested base-

The Mah-Jongg Craze

In 1923 the game of mah-jongg became the newest craze of the decade, selling more than 1.5 million sets.

Mah-jongg is similar to the card game rummy, but it uses tiles engraved with Chinese drawings and symbols. The tiles are divided into several categories, including dragons (which come in red, white, and green), winds, dots, craks, bams, flowers, and seasons. The object of the game is to form winning combinations of tiles to earn points.

Ma Chiang, the model for mah-jongg, had been played in China as early as 500 B.C. The entrepreneur Joseph Babcock combined aspects of that ancient game with aspects of American card games and patented mah-jongg in 1920.

ball at least a dozen years earlier and had grown, unchecked, to ravage the features of a generation."

In the wake of the scandal, desperate team owners decided to create the new position of commissioner of baseball. They appointed the well-respected Judge Kenesaw Mountain Landis to the post and ordered him to clean up the game.

Scandals were not the only problem facing baseball. Dwindling attendance for the previous seven years meant that fans were losing interest in the game. Baseball had become a game of pitching and defense. It was the "dead-ball" era, when the heavy ball had little carry

▲ Babe Ruth (left) and Lou Gehrig constituted the middle of the fearsome Yankees' batting lineup referred to as Murderers' Row. Most experts judge the 1927 Yankees to be the best baseball team in history.

RUTH'S RECORD

The compiling of sports statistics became the rage in the 1920s. One minister proclaimed: "If St. Paul were living today, he would know Babe Ruth's batting average." Ruth's numbers for just two years show his awesome achievements:

	1927	1928
Batting average	.356	.323
Home runs	60	54
Runs batted in	164	142

even when it was hit well. Home-run leaders often had no more than a dozen homers a year.

The ball was hard to see, too—both for the fans and the players—because of the tobacco and licorice juice players spit into their gloves, making the balls dark and dirty. To make matters worse, balls were rarely changed during games.

A New Image

Beginning in 1921, the rules were changed to keep the ball clean and make it livelier. Four years later, a new type of ball with a cushioned cork center was introduced. Suddenly, hitters began to spray baseballs all over the park, especially over the outfield fences. Batting averages jumped, and home-run totals soared. Fans loved the ac-

tion, and they returned to the ball-park—93 million during the 1920s, up more than 60 percent from the previous decade. The surge in attendance was helped by the rise of the New York Yankees and especially by the emergence of Babe Ruth as a superstar.

The Sultan of Swat

One of the greatest baseball players of all time was George Herman Ruth, nicknamed the Babe, the Bambino, and the Sultan of Swat. "After the Black Sox scandal," explained one sportswriter, "Babe Ruth with his bat pounded baseball back into popularity."

In 1920 the Boston Red Sox sold Ruth, a good-natured but often uncouth man, to the New York Yankees. Ruth promptly thrilled the entire nation by slugging 54 home runs, at that time an unheard-of number. The next year he showed his feat was no fluke by slugging 59 home runs. Then in 1927 he belted a record 60 homers, leading to a career total of 714, a record unsurpassed until broken by Henry Aaron in 1974.

Babe Ruth's power with a bat was astounding. An observer at the 1923 World Series, where Ruth hit three home runs, had this to say about one of the Babe's shots: "The ball started climbing from the moment it left the plate. It was a pop fly . . . and, though it flew high, it also flew far. When last seen the ball was crossing the roof of the stand in deep right field at an altitude of 315 feet. We wonder whether new baseballs conversing together in the original package ever remark, 'Join Ruth and see the world.'"

Ruth was the heart and soul of Murderers' Row, a powerful New York Yankee lineup that gained a well-deserved reputation in the 1920s for sending opposing pitchers to an early shower. After being terrorized by Ruth's fearsome bat, for example, a pitcher then had to face Lou Gehrig, who in 1927 batted .373 and belted 47 home runs. Gehrig earned a career batting average of .340, hit an average of 35 homers a year, and played outstanding defensive baseball at first base.

Together, Ruth and Gehrig formed a powerful one-two hitting punch. The Yankees had a record of 110 wins and only 44 losses in 1927, and they won the World Series from the Pittsburgh Pirates in four straight games. Most baseball experts regard the 1927 Yankees as the best team in the history of the game.

The Georgia Peach

Other teams also had talented stars. The man some experts consider the greatest all-around player in history was Ty Cobb, the "Georgia Peach." When Cobb first came to the Detroit Tigers to play center field in 1905, one writer described him as "a hick from Nowhere, Georgia, crude and unpolished."

Cobb may have been crude, but his baseball skills were anything but. He earned a career batting average of .367 and hit .300 or better 23 out of 24 years. An intimidating base runner, Cobb set a lifetime record of 892 stolen bases that stood until Lou Brock broke it in 1977. His record of 4,190 total base hits held up until Pete Rose surpassed it in 1985.

Horse Racing's Brightest Star: Man o' War

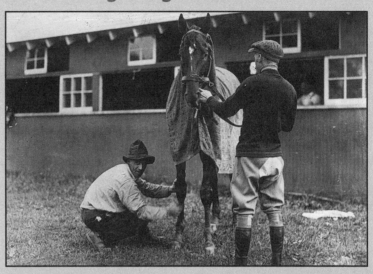

Man o' War, or "Big Red," as the sportswriters called him, weighed an amazing 1,150 pounds and ate so much that his groom resorted to feeding him with a bit in his mouth. Man o' War's huge stride measured 27 feet.

His size never slowed him down. In fact, the jockey's most difficult task was keeping "Big Red" in check when the horse wanted to run all out. Shortly after riding Man o' War for the first time, the leading jockey of the decade announced with awe, "That day, I knew I was riding the greatest horse ever bred for running."

Man o' War started 21 races in 1919 and 1920, winning all but one. Once he led the rest of the field by nearly 100 lengths at the finish. Three times the odds against his losing a race reached 100 to 1.

On July 10, 1920, Man o' War raced at Aqueduct in what the *New York Times* called "the greatest race of turf history." In the race, Man o' War trailed another superhorse named John P. Grier, and it seemed that Grier would win.

Man o' War's jockey was compelled to use his whip, and Man o' War "responded as the great horse he is. He charged at his rival with all the power of his marvelous frame and simply broke the heart of as game a three-year-old as this country will see in many a day." On that day, the *Times* concluded, "Man o' War proved himself the horse of eternity."

The Negro and Minor Leagues

Until Jackie Robinson broke baseball's color barrier in 1947, black athletes were not permitted to play in the major leagues. Nevertheless, the professional Negro Leagues featured some of the most talented baseball players of the day. One of the greatest was Oscar Charleston, who led the league in home runs three times between 1921 and 1933. Knowledgeable historians of the game think Charleston may have been as good a player as Ty Cobb, perhaps even better.

Minor-league baseball also thrived during the decade. Hundreds of minor-league teams delighted millions of fans, especially in areas outside the major-league cities of the Northeast and Midwest. America loved baseball once again, and everyone wanted to be a part of the game.

Football

COLLEGE FOOTBALL'S GREATEST LEGENDS

During the 1920s most of the widespread enthusiasm for football revolved around the college game, as played by powerful teams from Notre Dame, Michigan, Army, Southern California, and Minnesota, as well as Harvard, Princeton, and Yale. With radio stations broadcasting the games, millions of people across the nation caught football fever. By the end of the decade, more than 10 million people a year were climbing into the stands at college football games.

Knute Rockne

Football during the period had its full share of heroes—some coaches and some players. One of the most famous coaches of the decade was Knute Rockne. As a receiver at Notre Dame during the 1910s, Rockne and quarterback Gus Dorais changed the game of football dramatically by making the forward pass a potent offensive weapon.

In 1918 Rockne returned to Notre Dame as a coach. By 1931 he had compiled a record of 105 wins and only 12 losses—still the best winning percentage of any college coach. Rockne's teams responded to his superb coaching, especially his legendary inspirational talks at halftime. Perhaps Rockne's greatest talent, however, was his uncanny ability to find and train gifted players.

Four of Rockne's finest made up the backfield of the team that played Army on October 18, 1924. Grantland Rice, one of the decade's most celebrated sportswriters, covered the game and described for his readers the blazing speed and devastating impact of the Notre Dame backfield:

> Outlined against a blue-gray October sky, the Four Horsemen rode again. In dramatic lore they were known as Famine, Pestilence, Destruction, and Death. These are only aliases. Their real names are Stuhldreher, Miller, Crowley, and Layden. They formed the crest of the South Bend cyclone before which another fighting Army football team was swept over the precipice. . . .
>
> We doubt that any team in the country could have beaten Rockne's array yesterday afternoon, East or West. It was a great football team brilliantly directed, a team of speed,

power and team play. The Army has no cause for gloom over its showing. It played first-class football against more speed than it could match.

Those who have tackled a cyclone can understand.

Red Grange

Even Rockne's finest players were no match for Harold "Red" Grange, who played for the University of Illinois. A halfback, Grange carried the ball more often than most modern-day running backs. He was undoubtedly one of the speediest and most elusive football players in history.

His skill as a broken-field runner inspired Grantland Rice to call him the "Galloping Ghost." While at Illinois Grange rushed for 3,367 yards and scored 31 touchdowns. He was named an All-American three times.

One of Grange's most memorable games came in 1924 against the University of Michigan, supposedly a superior team. Grange ran for a touchdown each of the first four times he touched the ball, paving the way for a 39–14 upset of Michigan's Wolverines.

The Professional Game

Football was still a young professional sport when the American Professional Football Association (APFL) was founded. The APFL changed its name to the National Football League (NFL) in 1922.

Even with the legendary Jim Thorpe as its president, the NFL was a small-time operation. Franchises sold for as little as $50; games between the Chicago Bears and the New York Giants often drew fewer than 100 spectators.

◄ Red Grange was one of the best football players of all time. His entry into professional football put thousands into the stands for the first time—and made him a millionaire.

Then in 1925 Red Grange began to play professional football. Fans flocked to see the Galloping Ghost. They filled the stadiums wherever Grange played—36,000 in Chicago and 73,000 in New York. Grange earned about $1,000 a minute for playing the game. In three years, he was a millionaire.

By the end of the decade, many college players hoped to become professional, following in the footsteps of Grange. The NFL had become a successful enterprise.

Boxing

THE DEMPSEY-TUNNEY ERA

The national passion for what some called the "manly art" of prizefighting reached its peak during the 1920s. Five times between 1921 and 1927 American fans paid more than a million dollars to watch two men fight.

ALL-AMERICANS

Every year college football fans and players eagerly await the annual selection of players to the list of All-Americans. This means of recognizing the best offensive and defensive college players in the nation was started in 1889 by Walter Camp and Casper W. Whitney. Camp made so many contributions to the game that he is often considered the father of college football.

In 1927, however, 150,000 people paid nearly $2.7 million to see two men fight for just 45 minutes. According to the *New York Times,* the attendance figure was a sure sign of prosperity. It also showed how much Americans were willing to pay for a thrill.

And what a thrill! The match—between Jack Dempsey and Gene Tunney at Soldier Field, Chicago, on September 22, 1927—was the prizefight of the decade.

Jack Dempsey

Dempsey was a natural fighter, a warm and humorous man who had grown up in Manassa, Colorado, and had turned to boxing to make a buck. "He was a killer—a superhuman wild man" in the ring. "He was a fighter—one who used every trick to wreck the other fighter," wrote one sportswriter. Dempsey's powerful right hand and tenacious

style earned him the nickname the "Manassa Mauler."

In 1919 Dempsey knocked down defending champion Jess Willard seven times before knocking him out in the third round. When Dempsey defended the title in 1923 against Luis Firpo, the Argentine "Wild Bull of the Pampas," Firpo knocked the champ completely out of the ring. But sportswriters at ringside pushed Dempsey back into the ring, and the champ recovered to win by a knockout.

Gene Tunney

As a city kid who grew up in an apartment over a grocery store in New York City, Tunney was a different kind of fighter. He began fighting in neighborhood clubs. When World War I started, Tunney joined the Marines. Sent to Europe, he won the light-heavyweight championship of the Army Expeditionary Force.

He did other things as well, such as meeting with the playwright George Bernard Shaw and studying Shakespeare's *A Winter's Tale* until he knew "what was going on." Tunney turned to boxing because his fists were the best way out of a meager future in New York. He enjoyed the strategy of the ring, however, and made himself into a cool, calculating boxer.

The Match of the Decade

Tunney and Dempsey met in the ring for the first time in 1926, with Tunney winning the championship from Dempsey with relative ease. "What happened?" asked Dempsey's dismayed wife. "Honey, I forgot to duck," replied the for-

▼ Gene Tunney knocks Jack Dempsey to the canvas in the eighth round of their 1927 rematch.

mer champion, who was three years older than Tunney and perhaps past his prime.

Their 1927 return match was a memorable fight, less for its outcome than for the controversy surrounding it. Tunney was well in control when Dempsey made a sudden bid for victory in the seventh round. He lashed Tunney with two wicked punches to the jaw, and Tunney sank to the canvas, lying there for a full 15 seconds before the referee started counting.

Only when Dempsey moved to a neutral corner did the referee begin what many people called the "long count." Tunney struggled to his feet before the referee's count ended and went on to win the hotly debated match.

When Tunney retired in 1928, he was still the undefeated heavyweight champion of the world. Turning to other interests, Tunney became a successful businessman, wrote two books, and served in World War II. Dempsey retired after his defeat and became a successful sports promoter.

Tennis

TILDEN AND WILLS MAKE TENNIS BIG

Tennis changed from a quiet, country club sport into a major spectator attraction during the 1920s. Much of the credit for this dramatic rise in popularity belongs to two Americans, "Big Bill" Tilden and Helen Wills. Their dominance

▲ A showman on and off the court, Bill Tilden dominated tennis in the 1920s and made it popular with the American public.

of the game and Tilden's on-court showmanship created an entire new generation of tennis fans.

Master Showman
William Tatem Tilden was 27 years old before he won his first national singles championship in 1920. In the next ten years, however, Tilden stood alone at the top of the tennis world. He won ten of the major world singles titles, including six U.S. championships in a row and three wins at Wimbledon. He also led the United States tennis team to Davis Cup victories every year from 1920 to 1926.

To watch Tilden on the tennis court was to watch a master showman at work. In fact, he once said that "the player owes the gallery as much as an actor owes an audience."

In one match, Tilden won the first two sets easily, then lost the

HOCKEY NEWS
In 1924 Boston became the first American city to put a professional hockey team on the ice as a member of the National Hockey League. In 1929 the Boston Bruins won professional hockey's highest prize, the Stanley Cup.

American Helen Wills dominated women's competitive tennis during the 1920s. She won the singles title at Wimbledon eight times.

next two sets because he was too busy clowning around and entertaining the crowd. After he fell behind 5 games to 2 in the final set, Tilden decided the time had come for his dramatic comeback. He strolled over to the sideline, slowly removed his sweater for the first time, and poured a pitcher of ice water over his head. After drying his hands, Tilden returned to the court and played superb tennis to win the match.

Unfortunately, Tilden wanted to be an actor off the court as well. He sank a sizable portion of his earnings into producing plays—starring himself, of course. All of his plays failed miserably. No one minded, however; his brilliant tennis was theater enough.

No-Nonsense Tennis

Helen Wills dominated women's tennis just as completely as Tilden dominated the men's game, but she was very different in her style

of play. Tilden was a showman. Wills was known as "Little Miss Poker Face" for her expressionless, methodical play. Tilden won his first championship at age 27. Wills won hers at age 17 in 1923.

Wills's statistics were even more impressive than Tilden's. She won Wimbledon eight times, the U.S. championship seven times, and the French championship four times. She also won three doubles titles at Wimbledon and four at the U.S. championships. Between 1927 and 1930, Wills won every match she entered, losing only a single set in the process.

Wills used her powerful serve to wear out her opponents and her bulletlike ground strokes to finish them off. Of her victory at Wimbledon in 1927, *Time* magazine wrote:

> Miss Wills, smashing like clockwork, seemed to have regained and even surpassed the magnificent speed and rallying power which she possessed before her operation for appendicitis. . . . Putting her strokes like pistol shots, Miss Wills took the eighth game, the ninth, the tenth. Then she was the women's singles champion at Wimbledon—and, by popular consent, women's singles champion of the world.

Golf

THE LEGENDARY BOBBY JONES

Like other sports in the 1920s, the game of golf saw tremendous growth. The increase in the number of golf courses nationwide led directly to more men and women playing the game. Golf was less a spectator sport than other sports of the 1920s. Nevertheless, its growing popularity was fed by masters of the game who became heroes of the decade.

Bobby Jones

A golfing legend of the 1920s, Robert Tyre "Bobby" Jones ranks among the greatest golfers ever to stroll down a fairway. Between 1923 and 1929, Jones won 13 of the 27 major tournaments he entered. He won the U.S. Open three times, the U.S. Amateur Championship four times, and the British Open twice.

Jones was the first player ever to win the U.S. Open and the British Open in the same year. And in 1930, Jones won the British Amateur, British Open, U.S. Amateur, and U.S. Open—the "Grand Slam" of golf. No one had ever done it before, and no one has done it since. Ironically, the best golfer in history never turned professional.

Because of his accomplishments, Bobby Jones quickly became an idol to adoring golf fans in the United States and around the world. After Jones had won the Grand Slam, sportswriter Grantland Rice penned this tribute:

> There is no secret connected with Bobby Jones' mastery of the golf world. There are others who have a swing just about as sound, the same determination and the same ability to concentrate. But there is no other who has the all-around combination of these essential elements. This combination happened to meet in one man for the first time in the history of golf.

Jones retired from golf in 1930 to practice law. Every golfer who has since followed in his footsteps has played in the shadow of his legendary accomplishments.

Other Golfing Greats

The 1920s had other remarkable players. Between 1919 and 1929, the flamboyant Walter Hagen won ten major championships. Hagen won the U.S. Open once, the British Open four times, and the Professional Golfers' Association (PGA) Championship five times, including four straight. Hagen was also a major force in turning golf into a professional sport.

During the same period, Gene Sarazen won the U.S. Open once and the PGA twice. Both Hagen and Sarazen remained prominent players long after the 1920s had ended.

Philadelphian Glenna Collett was the foremost American woman golfer of the 1920s. She won the American championship six times and the Canadian title twice.

◀ Glenna Collett was the best American woman golfer of the 1920s.

Jones and Ruth: Sporting Styles of the Decade

Bobby Jones and Babe Ruth were both idols of an era, but that was about all they had in common. In his youth, Bobby Jones had an all-American boy image, clean-cut and polite. There was no indication he would become a sports star. As a child, recurring health problems gave little hope that he would play baseball like his father, who was once offered a professional contract by the Brooklyn Dodgers.

But young Bobby made up in energy and determination for his lack of interest in baseball. Turning to golf, he developed a flawless style and precise, grooved swing that became the envy of golfers on two continents.

Although he had a fiery temper, Jones learned that the secret to controlling his game was keeping his emotions in check. It was not an easy lesson for the talented golfer who failed to win a single tournament over a period of seven years. But Jones placed his frustration firmly behind him by aquiring a mastery of the mental aspects of the game.

Said one sportswriter who covered all of Jones's major tournaments, "Competitive golf is played mainly on a five-and-a-half-inch course, the space between the ears. This is where Jones excelled."

Babe Ruth, on the other hand, had a booming bat, a booming voice, and a booming way of life. Modesty was not one of his many virtues. "Shucks, I coulda hit a six hundred lifetime average easily," he once boasted with characteristic confidence. "But I woulda had to hit them singles. The people were payin' to see me hit

them home runs." To hold all of his fans, the Yankees opened a new stadium in 1923, often called "the house that Ruth built."

Ruth's passion for food was almost as intense as his love of baseball. His usual breakfast consisted of a Porterhouse steak, four fried eggs, and fried potatoes, all washed down with a pot of coffee and a pint of bourbon and ginger ale. His favorite snack between games of a doubleheader was a quart of chocolate ice cream and a jar of pickled eels. All in all, said the writer Jimmy Breslin, Babe Ruth is "the only sports legend I ever saw who completely lived up to advance billing."

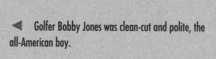

◀ Golfer Bobby Jones was clean-cut and polite, the all-American boy.

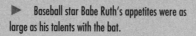

▶ Baseball star Babe Ruth's appetites were as large as his talents with the bat.

Swimming

THE CHAMPION AND THE CHANNEL SWIMMER

Johnny Weissmuller completely dominated men's competitive swimming during the 1920s. His career as a competitive swimmer stretched from 1921 to 1929. During that time he never lost a free-style race at distances from 100 yards to half a mile.

As handsome as he was swift, Weissmuller was the first swimmer to win five gold medals in the Olympic Games: the 100-meter freestyle and 800-meter freestyle relay in both 1924 and 1928 and the 400-meter freestyle in 1924.

Weissmuller won 51 U.S. national championships and set 67 world records during his eight-year career. In 1950, 250 sportswriters voted him the greatest swimmer of the first half of the twentieth century. He retired from competition at the age of 24 to become a jungle hero, playing Tarzan in a number of Hollywood movies, including *Tarzan the Ape Man* (1932) and *Tarzan Escapes* (1936).

Gertrude Ederle set almost 30 national and world records as a competitive swimmer and won three medals at the 1924 Olympics. But she made front-page news in 1926 when she became the first woman to swim the English Channel. In successfully crossing the channel, her time of 14 hours and 31 minutes was almost two hours faster than the men's record.

A proud nation honored "Our Trudy" with a huge ticker-tape parade in New York. "If there is one woman who can make the swim," wrote one journalist before her bold attempt, "it is this girl, with the shoulders and back of Jack Dempsey and the frankest and bravest pair of eyes that ever looked into a face."

As in all such times, the petty conventional life of the city went on, ignoring the [Russian] Revolution as much as possible. The poets made verses—but not about the Revolution. The realistic painters painted scenes from medieval Russian history—anything but the Revolution. . . . The ladies of the minor bureaucratic set took tea with each other in the afternoon, carrying each her little gold or silver or jewelled sugar-box, and half a loaf of bread in her muff, and wished that the Tsar were back, or that the Germans would come, or anything that would solve the servant problem. . . . The daughter of a friend of mine came home one afternoon in hysterics because the woman street-car conductor had called her 'Comrade!'

—John Reed,
Ten Days That Shook the World, 1919

The basic freedom of the world is woman's freedom. A free race cannot be born of slave mothers. A woman enchained cannot choose but give a measure of that bondage to her sons and daughters. No woman can call herself free who does not own and control her body. No woman can call herself free until she can choose consciously whether she will or will not be a mother.

—Margaret Sanger,
Woman and the New Race,
1920

RUTH BOUGHT BY NEW YORK AMERICANS FOR $125,000

Highest Price in Baseball Annals

—*New York Times,* January 6, 1920

"America's present need is not heroics but healing; not nostrums but normalcy; not revolution but restoration; not surgery but serenity."

—Warren G. Harding,
campaign speech, 1920

No person shall, on or after the date when the Eighteenth Amendment to the Constitution of the United States goes into effect, manufacture, sell, barter, transport, import, export, deliver, furnish or possess any intoxicating liquor except as authorized in this act.

—From the National Prohibition Act, 1919

My candle burns at both ends;
It will not last the night;
But, ah, my foes, and, oh, my friends—
It gives a lovely light.

—Edna St. Vincent Millay,
from *A Few Figs from Thistles,* 1920

"It is the dull man who is always sure, and the sure man who is always dull."

—H. L. Mencken, 1920

VOICES OF THE ERA

I pledge allegiance to the flag of the United States of America and to the Republic for which it stands, one nation, indivisible, with liberty and justice for all.

—The Pledge of Allegiance, as revised in 1924

56 is just a number—
58 is just a number—
but 57 means good things to eat

—H. J. Heinz Company ad, 1923

"I do not like women who know too much.**"**

—Rudolph Valentino, 1922

"Since the Crusades I do not know of any enterprise which has done more honor to men than the intervention of America in the War.**"**

—C. de Wiert, prime minister of Belgium, 1921

To George F. Babbitt, as to most prosperous citizens of Zenith, his motor car was poetry and tragedy, love and heroism. The office was his pirate ship but the car his perilous excursion ashore.

—Sinclair Lewis, *Babbitt*, 1922

That's my man,
    I want him for my own.
No! No! He's my sweet daddy,
    You'd better leave that man alone.
See that suit he's got on?
    I bought it last week.
I've been buyin' clothes for five years
    for that is my black sheik.
I guess we got to have him
    on cooperation plan.
I guess we got to have him
    on cooperation plan.
Bessie! Clara! Ain't nothin' diff'rent
    'bout that rotten two-time man.

—Bessie Smith,
"My Man Blues," 1925

Often a bridesmaid
but never a bride
For Halitosis use
Listerine

—Listerine mouthwash ad, 1924

"Men seldom make passes
At girls who wear glasses.**"**

—Dorothy Parker, 1920s

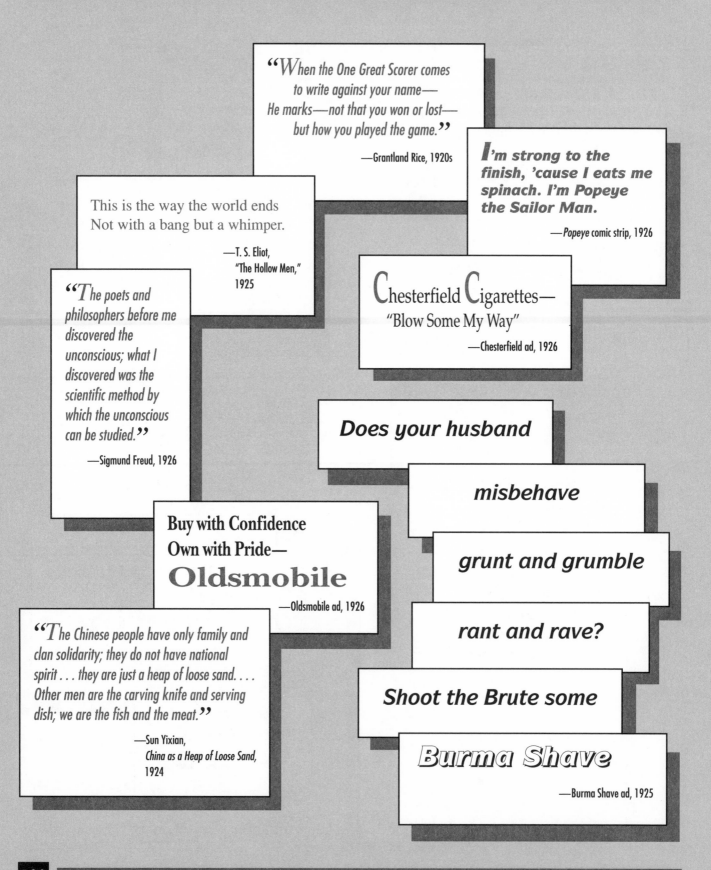

"When the One Great Scorer comes
to write against your name—
He marks—not that you won or lost—
but how you played the game."

—Grantland Rice, 1920s

I'm strong to the
finish, 'cause I eats me
spinach. I'm Popeye
the Sailor Man.

—Popeye comic strip, 1926

This is the way the world ends
Not with a bang but a whimper.

—T. S. Eliot,
"The Hollow Men,"
1925

"The poets and
philosophers before me
discovered the
unconscious; what I
discovered was the
scientific method by
which the unconscious
can be studied."

—Sigmund Freud, 1926

Chesterfield Cigarettes—
"Blow Some My Way"

—Chesterfield ad, 1926

Does your husband

misbehave

grunt and grumble

rant and rave?

Buy with Confidence
Own with Pride—
Oldsmobile

—Oldsmobile ad, 1926

"The Chinese people have only family and
clan solidarity; they do not have national
spirit . . . they are just a heap of loose sand. . . .
Other men are the carving knife and serving
dish; we are the fish and the meat."

—Sun Yixian,
China as a Heap of Loose Sand,
1924

Shoot the Brute some

Burma Shave

—Burma Shave ad, 1925

VOICES OF THE ERA

I had seen nothing sacred, and the things that were glorious had no glory and the sacrifices were like the stockyards at Chicago if nothing was done with the meat except to bury it. . . . Abstract words such as glory, honor, courage, or hallow were obscene.

—Ernest Hemingway,
A Farewell to Arms, 1929

A chicken in every pot, a car in every garage.

—Republican political slogan, 1928

"*Not only am I innocent of these two crimes, not only in all my life I have never stole, never killed, never spilled blood, but I have struggled all my life, since I began to reason, to eliminate crime from the earth.*"

—Bartolomeo Vanzetti, 1927

*Your cares and troubles are gone;
There'll be no more from now on.
Happy days are here again,
The skies above are clear again;
Let us sing a song of cheer again
Happy days are here again!*

—Milton Ager and Jack Yellen,
"Happy Days Are Here Again," 1929

"*Moving pictures need sound as much as Beethoven symphonies need lyrics.*"

—Charles Chaplin, 1928

"*You ain't heard nothin' yet, folks.*"

—Al Jolson
in the film
The Jazz Singer, 1927

My soul has grown deep like the rivers.

—Langston Hughes,
"The Negro Speaks of Rivers," 1926

I believe that on the first night I went to Gatsby's house I was one of the few guests who had actually been invited. People were not invited—they went there. They got into automobiles which bore them out to Long Island, and somehow they ended up at Gatsby's door. Once there they were introduced by somebody who knew Gatsby, and after that they conducted themselves according to the rules of behavior associated with amusement parks. Sometimes they came and went without having met Gatsby at all, came for the party with a simplicity of heart that was its own ticket of admission.

—F. Scott Fitzgerald,
The Great Gatsby, 1925

Glossary

anarchist: a person who believes that all forms of government authority are undesirable and should be abolished

antibiotic: a drug that fights and destroys bacterial infections and is widely used to treat and prevent diseases

bootlegging: the practice of making, selling, or transporting alcoholic beverages unlawfully

boycott: to refuse to use, buy, or deal with something in order to express disapproval

business cycle: the recurring movement of the economy from good times to bad times and back again in four stages: prosperity, recession, depression, and recovery

capitalism: an economic system controlled by individuals and corporations rather than by government, characterized by open competition in a free market

Central Powers: during World War I, the countries that fought against the Allies, including Germany, Austria-Hungary, Bulgaria, and Turkey

civil disobedience: refusal to obey laws as a matter of conscience and a means of influence

collective farm: a farm or group of farms organized and worked by a group of laborers under government supervision

collective security: security for nations, achieved by the formation of an international organization for peace or of a group of allied nations

colonialism: the control of one nation over a dependent area or people

covenant: a formal agreement or contract

Dow-Jones industrial average: an index of the price of stocks based on the daily average price of selected industrial, transportation, and utility stocks

inflation: a general increase in prices and fall in the purchasing value of money in an economy

lynching: an execution carried out by a mob without due process of law

mandate: an authorization to take action as a representative of an organized body

Progressive: a person who believes that political and social reforms will improve life and that the government should protect the public interest

Prohibition: the period (1922–1933) during which the production, manufacture, and sale of alcoholic beverages was illegal in the United States

purge: to rid a nation, political party, or other group of persons who are considered undesirable

recession: a temporary decline in economic activity

relativity: Einstein's theory stating that all motion is relative and time is a fourth dimension related to space

reparations: compensation that a victor demands from a defeated enemy for war damages

socialism: an economic theory that promotes governmental control of factories and other businesses

speculation: the act of taking financial risks in the hope of making a large profit

suffrage: the right to vote

tabloid: a small-format newspaper that gives the news in condensed form, usually with illustrated, often sensational material

Zionism: a movement founded by the Jewish people to establish a homeland in Palestine

Suggested Readings

General

Abbott, Carl. *Urban America in the Modern Age, 1920 to Present.* H. Davidson, 1987.

Allen, Frederick Lewis. *The Big Change, 1900–1950.* Bantam, 1965.

Blum, Daniel. *A Pictorial History of the Silent Screen.* Grosset & Dunlap, 1953.

Cairns, Trevor. *The Twentieth Century.* Cambridge University Press, 1984.

Cantor, Norman F., and Michael S. Werthman, eds. *The History of Popular Culture.* Macmillan, 1968.

Churchill, Allen. *The Great White Way.* E. P. Dutton, 1962.

Daniels, Roger. *Coming to America: A History of Immigration and Ethnicity in American Life.* HarperCollins, 1990.

Davids, Jules. *America and the World of Our Time.* Random House, 1960.

Ewing, Elizabeth. *History of Twentieth Century Fashion.* Barnes & Noble, 1986.

Filene, Peter G. *Him/Her/Self: Sex Roles in Modern America.* Johns Hopkins University Press, 1986.

Flink, James J. *The Automobile Age.* MIT, 1988.

Freidel, Frank. *America in the Twentieth Century.* Knopf, 1960.

Goff, Richard. *The Twentieth Century: A Brief Global History.* John Wiley, 1983.

Hine, Darlene Clark, ed. *Black Women in American History.* Carlson Publishing, 1990.

Manchester, William. *The Glory and the Dream: A Narrative History of America, 1932–1972.* Little, Brown, 1974.

May, George S., ed. *The Automobile Industry, 1920–1980.* Facts on File, 1989.

Morgan, Robert P. *Twentieth-Century Music: A History of Musical Style in Modern Europe and America.* Norton, 1991.

Noble, David W., David A. Horowitz, and Peter N. Carroll. *Twentieth Century Limited: A History of Recent America.* Houghton Mifflin, 1980.

Norman, Philip. *The Road Goes On Forever: Portraits from a Journey Through Contemporary Music.* Simon & Schuster, 1982.

Olderman, Murray. *Nelson's Twentieth Century Encyclopedia of Baseball.* Nelson, 1963.

Oliver, John W. *History of American Technology.* Books on Demand UMI, 1956.

Ritter, Lawrence S. *The Story of Baseball.* Morrow, 1983.

Sklar, Robert. *Movie-Made America: A Cultural History of American Movies.* Random House, 1976.

Spaeth, Sigmund. *A History of Popular Music in America.* Random House, 1948.

Susman, Warren I. *Culture as History: The Transformation of American Society in the Twentieth Century.* Pantheon, 1984.

Taft, Philip. *Organized Labor in American History.* Harper & Row, 1964.

Vecsey, George, ed. *The Way It Was: Great Sports Events from the Past.* McGraw-Hill, 1974.

Zinn, Howard. *The Twentieth Century: A People's History.* Harper & Row, 1984.

About the Era

Abels, Jules. *In the Time of Silent Cal.* Putnam, 1969.

Allen, Frederick Lewis. *Only Yesterday: An Informal History of the 1920s.* HarperCollins, 1991.

Bender, David L., and Bruno Leone. *Science and Religion: Opposing Viewpoints.* Greenhaven, 1981.

Chalmers, David M. *Hooded Americanism: The History of the Ku Klux Klan,* 2nd ed. Franklin Watts, 1981.

Daniels, Jonathan. *The Time Between the Wars.* Doubleday, 1966.

Dank, Milton. *Albert Einstein.* Franklin Watts, 1983.

Franklin, Joe. *Classics of the Silent Screen.* Citadel, 1959.

Galbraith, John Kenneth. *The Great Crash: 1929.* Houghton Mifflin, 1955.

Ginger, Ray. *Six Days or Forever? Tennessee v. John Thomas Scopes.* Oxford University Press, 1974.

Goldston, Robert. *The Road Between the Wars: 1918–1941.* Dial, 1978.

Huggins, Nathan. *Harlem Renaissance.* Oxford University Press, 1973.

Murray, Robert K. *The Red Scare: A Study in National Hysteria.* McGraw-Hill, 1955.

Perrett, Geoffrey. *America in the Twenties: A History.* Simon & Schuster, 1982.

Sinclair, Andrew. *Prohibition: The Era of Excess.* Little, Brown, 1962.

Index

Note: A page number in italic indicates a table, map, graph, or illustration.

Aaron, Henry, 108
Abie's Irish Rose, 95
Abzug, Bella, 24
Academy of Motion Picture Arts and Sciences, 99–100
Advertising, 19–20, 28, 33, 66–67, 80–81, 98
AFL-CIO, 61
Africa, 55–56
African-Americans. *See also* Race relations
  Harlem Renaissance and, 89–91
  labor movement and, 61
  migration to North, 17–19
  music and, 87–89
  in sports, 110, 112
  vote and, 22
Age of Innocence, The, 93
Agricultural Marketing Act, 71
Aircraft, *75,* 77–79
Akhmatova, Anna, 41
Allies, 12, 40, 45. *See also* World War I
American Civil Liberties Union (ACLU), 85
American Farm Bureau Federation, 71
American Federation of Labor (AFL), 61
American Mercury magazine, 94
American Professional Football Association (APFL), 111
American Temperance Society, 25
Amos 'n' Andy, 80, 101
Amundsen, Roald, 79
Anderson, Sherwood, 85
Angelus Temple, 97
Anna Christie, 96
Anna Karenina, 99
Anthony, Susan B., 22
Antibiotics, 82–83
Antievolution bills, 84–85
Anti-Saloon League, 25, 26
Arabs, Palestine Problem and, 49–53
Architecture, 103
Argentina, 56
Armenia, 39, 51
Armstrong, Louis "Satchmo," 88, 89
Army football team, 110
Art, 90, 102–103
Art Deco, 103
Asia Minor, 51
Asians, 32
Assembly lines, 63, 75–76
Astaire, Adele, 95
Astaire, Fred, 95
Atatürk, Kemal, 51
Austria-Hungary, 37

Automobile industry, 63, 68–69, 76, *76*
Automobiles, 67–70

Babbitt, 92
Babcock, Joseph, 107
Balfour, Lord Arthur James, 50–51
Balfour Declaration, 51–52, *52,* 53
Balloons, 79
Banking, 45–46, 64, 72
Bank of Manhattan, 19
Banting, Frederick, 82
Baptism in Kansas, 102
Barnstorming, 77
Barrymore, John, 100
Barton, Bruce, 66–67
Baseball, 107–110
Bauhaus style, 103
Beau Brummel, 100
Beiderbecke, Bix, 89
Bell, Alexander Graham, 32
Bella Donna, 100
Belorussia, 42
Best, Charles, 82
Big Four (Paris Peace Conference), 12
Big Three automakers, 68
Black Sox scandal, 107
Black Star Line, 18
Black Thursday, 73
Blue-collar workers, 19–20, 60–61
Blue Cross, 62
Blues, 89
Blue Shield, 62
Bob's Party Number One, 103
Bohr, Niels, 83
Bolden, Buddy, 88
Bolshevik Revolution, 41, 42, 44
Book-of-the-Month Club (BOMC), 93
Books, 49, 90, 92–93, 94, 106
Bootlegging, 26–27, 29
Boston, 113
Bow, Clara, 99
Boxing, 111–113
Brazil, 56
Breslin, Jimmy, 116
Brest-Litovsk, Treaty of, 42, 43
Britain, 32, 40
  economy of, 45
  Egypt and, 52
  India and, 54–55
  Palestine and, 52–53
  World War I and, 12, 36, 37, 45, 46, 50, 55
Broadway, 89, 95–96
Brock, Lou, 109
Brotherhood of Sleeping Car Porters, 61
Bryan, William Jennings, 85
Bulgaria, 38
Bunford, 31

Bush, George, 32
Business, 13, 16, 60, 72. *See also* Advertising; Commerce; Trade
  assembly line and, 75–76
  automobile industry and, 63, 68–69, 76, *76*
  black, 18
  corporations and, 62–63
  labor and, 19–20
  unions and, 61–62
  after World War I, 45, 46
Business cycle, 59
Butler Act, 84–85
Byrd, Richard E., 78–79

Camille, 99
Camp, Walter, 111
Canada, 32
Cantos, 93–94
Capone, Al, 26
Carnarvon, Lord (George Edward Stanhope Molyneux), 81
Carrel, Dr. Alexis, 82
Carrel suture, 82
Carter, Howard, 81
Carter, Jimmy, 32
Catt, Carrie Chapman, 22, 23–24
Central Powers, 49. *See also* World War I
Certain People of Importance, 93
Chain, Ernst, 82–83
Chaplin, Charlie, 98
Charleston, Oscar, 110
Chicago, 18
China, 53–54
Chinese Communist party, 54
Chisholm, Shirley, 24
Chrysler, Walter P., 68
Chrysler Building, 19, 103
Chrysler Corporation, 68
Churchill, Winston, 53
Citibank, 64
Civil disobedience, 55
Clarke, Edward Y., 33
Class divisions, in U.S., 20, 21–22, 60
Classical music, 102
Clemenceau, Georges, 12, 36, 37, 38
Cleveland, 18
Cliquot Club Eskimos, 102
Cobb, Ty, 109
Coca-Cola, 28
Collective farms, 44
College football, 110–111
Collett, Glenna, 115
Columbia Broadcasting Company, 81
Columbia Broadcasting System (CBS), 81
Commerce, 62–64. *See also* Business; Trade

Commercial Cable Company, 79
Communism, 41, 42, 54
  Red Scare and, 30–31
  War Communism and, 42–43
Communist party, 43, 54
Computing-Tabulating-Recording Company, 69
Connie's Inn, 89
Constitution, U.S.
  Eighteenth Amendment to, 24, 26
  Fifteenth Amendment to, 22
  Fourteenth Amendment to, 22
  Nineteenth Amendment to, 23
Consumer goods, 19–20, 63, 64–65
Coolidge, Calvin, 13, 15–16, 56, 60, 66, 71
Corporations, 62–63. *See also* Business
Costa Rica, 56
Cotton Club, 89
Council of People's Commissars, 42
Cox, James M., 13
Crawford, Joan, 100
Credit, 65–66, 72–73
Creole Jazz Band, 88, 89
Crime, 26
Crossword puzzles, 106
Cuba, 57
Cullen, Countee, 90
Culture, 89–91
cummings, e. e., 93
Curry, John Steuart, 102
Czechoslovakia, 37, 46

Dance, 89, 96–97
Darwin, Charles, 85
Daugherty, Harry, 14
Dawes, Charles G., 49
De Mille, Cecil B., 100
Dempsey, Jack, 112–113
Depression, defined, 59. *See also* Great Depression
Detroit, 18, 33
De Valera, Eamon, 47
Diabetes, 82
Dinner for Threshers, 102
Dirigibles, 79
Disneyland, 98
Disney World, 98
Dodge, 68
Dollar diplomacy, 56
Dominican Republic, 57
Douglas, Aaron, 90
Dow-Jones industrial average, 63–64
Drama, 90, 96
Dreyfus, Alfred, 50
Du Bois, W. E. B., 90
Duncan, Isadora, 96, 100

Dzugashvili, Joseph. See Stalin, Joseph

Earthquakes, in Japan, 53
Easter Rebellion, 47
Economy, 11, 17–22, 59–62, 70–73
    World War I and, 36, 45–46, 59, 64
Ederle, Gertrude, 117
Education
    of managers, 63
    in Turkey, 51
Egypt, 52
Eighteenth Amendment, 24, 26
Einstein, Albert, 83
Einstein, "Izzy," 28–29
Elections. See also Vote
    presidential, 13–14, 16, 23, 57, 80
Electric appliances, 65, 76–77
Electricity, 63
Electric-powered machines, 63
Eliot, T. S., 94
Ellington, Edward "Duke," 89, 102
Emergency Quota Act (1919), 31
Emperor Jones, The, 96
Employment, 19–20, 21–22. See also Labor movement; Unemployment
    of blacks, 17
    of women, 22–23, 62
    workforce and, 60–62
England. See Britain
English Channel, 117
Estonia, 37
Eustis, Dorothy Harrison, 73
Evangelists, 97
Evans, Hiram Wesley, 33
Evolutionary biology, 84–85

Fads, 107
Fairbanks, Douglas, 100
Fair Employment Practices Committee, 61
Fall, Albert, 14–15
Famines, in USSR, 41
Farming, 21, 60, 71, 71
    collective, 44
    Russian, 41
    after World War I, 45, 46
Fascism, 48
Fashion, 106–107
Faulkner, William, 93
Federal Bureau of Investigation (FBI), 30
Federal Communications Commission, 80
Federal Farm Board, 72
Federal Radio Commission, 80
Feminine Mystique, The, 24
Ferber, Edna, 96
Ferguson, Miriam "Ma," 24
Fianna Fáil, 47
Fifteenth Amendment, 22
Finland, 37, 42
Firpo, Luis, 112
"First Fig," 94

Fitzgerald, F. Scott, 92, 93
Five-Power Treaty, 40
Five-Year Plans, 43–44
Flaherty, Robert, 100
Flappers, 106
Fleming, Alexander, 82
Flesh and the Devil, 100
Florey, Howard, 82–83
Food Administration, 59, 64
Football, 110–111
Ford, Henry, 64, 68–69, 75–76
Ford Motor Company, 18, 61, 68, 77
Fordson tractor, 71
Ford Trimotor, 77
Four-Power Treaty, 40
Fourteen Points, 12, 35–36
Fourteenth Amendment, 22
France, 32, 40
    Arab resistance and, 53
    economy of, 36, 45
    League of Nations and, 38
    World War I and, 12, 36, 37, 45, 46–47, 51, 55
French Canadians, 33
Freshman, The, 99
Friedan, Betty, 24, 100
Frost, Robert, 94
Fuad I, king of Egypt, 52
Fuel Administration, 59
Funny Face, 95

Gallico, Paul, 105
Galloping Gaucho, 98
Gandhi, Mohandas K. (Mahatma), 55
Gangsters, 26
Garbo, Greta, 99, 100
Garvey, Marcus, 18, 56
Gaylor, Wood, 103
Gaynor, Janet, 99–100
Gehrig, Lou, 109
General, The, 99
General Motors (GM), 68, 69
Geneva, Switzerland, 37
Georgia (country), 42
Germany, 32
    economy of, 45–46
    League of Nations and, 38
    unemployment in, 35
    war reparations and, 12, 36, 37, 45, 48
    World War I and, 37, 38, 40, 48–49, 55
Gershwin, George, 89, 95
Glenn, John H., Jr., 32
Glyn, Elinor, 99
Goddard, Robert, 79
Gold Rush, The, 98
Golf, 114–115
Good Neighbor policy, 57
Government of Ireland Act (1920), 47
Graham, Martha, 96–97
Grand Hotel, 99
Grand Ole Opry, 101
Grange, Harold "Red," 105, 111
Great Atlantic and Pacific Tea Co. (A&P), 67
Great Britain. See Britain
Great Depression, 45, 72–73

Great Gatsby, The, 92
Greece, 38, 51
Gropius, Walter, 103
Gross national product, in 1919–1929, 11
Guest, Edgar A., 94
Guide dogs, 73
Guomindang (Nationalist party), 54

Hadden, Brian, 95
Hagen, Walter, 114
Haley, Alex, 100
Hammerstein, Oscar, II, 96
Handy, W. C., 89
Hardin, Lillian, 89
Harding, Warren G., 13–15, 16, 60, 101
Hardy, Oliver, 99
Harlem Renaissance, 89–91
Harper's Bazaar, 94
Heisenberg, Werner, 84
Hemingway, Ernest, 93
Henderson, Fletcher, 89–90
Hertz, John, 70
Herzl, Theodor, 50
Hitler, Adolf, 48
Hockey, 113
Holland, Clifford M., 76
Holland Tunnel, 76
Home Rule Bill, 47
Home to Harlem, 91
Hoover, Herbert, 14, 16, 24, 57, 59, 60, 63, 71, 73
Hoover, J. Edgar, 30
Horse racing, 109
Horthy, Admiral Miklós, 46
Hot Five, 88
Hot Seven, 88
Houdini, Harry, 100
Household appliances, 65, 76–77
Hubbard, William DeHart, 112
Hubble, Edwin, 84
Hubble Space Telescope, 84
Hughes, Charles Evans, 14, 39
Hughes, Langston, 91
Hungary, 37
Hurston, Zora Neale, 90
Hussein, Faisal, 51
Hussein, Sharif, 50
Hyatt Roller Bearing Company, 69

Ibn Saud, king of Saudi Arabia, 52
Ice hockey, 113
"If We Must Die," 91
Il Duce. See Mussolini, Benito
Income taxes, 16
India, 54–55
Indianapolis, 33
Industrialization, 29, 68–69
    Russian, 43–44
Infectious diseases, 82–83
Inflation, 36, 45–46
Installment purchasing, 65–66
Insulin, 82
International Business Machines (IBM), 69

International Church of Foursquare Gospel, 97
International Court of Justice, 38
International trade, 46, 56
Inventions, 77, 82
Iran, 52
Iraq, 53
Ireland, 32, 47
Irish Free State, 47
Irish Republican Army (IRA), 47
Irish Republican Brotherhood, 47
It, 99
Italy, 32, 40
    economy of, 45
    World War I and, 12, 36, 37, 45, 47–48, 51

J. C. Penney, 67
Jannings, Emil, 99
Japan, 40, 53
    China and, 54
    modernization of, 53
    World War I and, 36, 37
Japanese-Americans, 33
Jazz, 87–89, 102
Jazz Singer, The, 100
Jews
    anti-Semitism and, 33, 50
    Palestine Problem and, 49–53
Jiang Jie-shi (Chiang Kai-shek), 54
Job, The, 62
John P. Grier (racehorse), 109
Jolson, Al, 100
Jones, Robert Tyre "Bobby," 114, 116
Jordan Motor Cars, 66
Joyce, James, 94
Julius's Annex, 103

KDKA, 80
Keaton, Buster, 99
Kellogg-Briand Pact (1928), 40
Kelly, "Shipwreck," 107
Kern, Jerome, 96
Khomeini, Ayatollah Ruhollah, 52
Kid Brother, The, 99
Kiernan, John, 105, 106
King, Martin Luther, Jr., 32
King Tut's tomb, 81
Knopf, Alfred, 91
Kreisler, Fritz, 88
Ku Klux Klan (KKK), 32–33

Labor movement, 19–20
    Red Scare and, 30–31, 61
Lady Be Good! 95
Landis, Judge Kenesaw Mountain, 107
Lardner, Ring, 105
Latin America, 56–57
Latvia, 37
Laurel, Stan, 99
Lazarus, Emma, 32
League of Nations, 11, 12–13, 37, 38–39, 55

League of Women Voters, 24
Leisure, 69–70, 106–107
Lenin, Vladimir Ilyich, 40, 41–43
Lewis, Sinclair, 62, 92
Liberty Bonds, 64
Life magazine, 94
Lindbergh, Charles A., 78, 82, 101
Lindsay, Vachel, 91
Lithuania, 37
Living standard, 20, 65–66, *66*
Lloyd, Harold, 98–99
Lloyd George, David, 12, 36
Locke, Alain, 90
Lodge, Henry Cabot, 12–13, 32
Lopez, Vincent, 102
Lost generation, 93
Luce, Henry, 95
Lucky Strike cigarettes, 66
Lynchings, 31–33

Ma Chiang (Chinese game), 107
McKay, Claude, 91
McNamee, Graham, 101
McNary-Haugen Bill, 71
McPherson, Aimee Semple, 96, 97
Magazines, 93, 94, 95
Mah-jongg, 107
Mail service, 77
Main Street, 92
Management, 63
Man Nobody Knows, The, 66
Man o' War, 109
Mao Ze-dong (Mao Tse-tung), 54
Marble Faun, The, 93
March on Washington for Jobs and Freedom, 61
Marconi, Guglielmo, 79
Marconi Wireless Telegraph Company, 79
Marsh, Reginald, 103
Marx, Karl, 43, 44
Maxwell Company, 68
May Fourth Movement, 53–54
Medical insurance, 62
Medicine, 81–83
Mein Kampf, 49
Mellon, Andrew, 14, 16, 73
Mencken, H. L., 92–93, 94, 105
Messenger magazine, 61
Mexican-Americans, 33
Mexico, 32, 56, 57
Mickey Mouse, 98
Middle East, 49–53, *50*
Miës van der Rohe, Ludwig, 103
Migration, 17–19
 to cities, 29
Millay, Edna St. Vincent, 94
Minor-league baseball, 110
Miss America contest, 106
Mitchell, William L. "Billy," 77
Model A Ford, 69
Model T Ford, 65, 69, 75–76

Modernism, 103
Molyneux, George Edward Stanhope (Lord Carnarvon), 81
Monarchies, 52
Montague, Edwin, 54
Montague-Chelmsford Reforms, 54
Moran, Bugs, 27
Morocco, 56
Morrow, Dwight, 57
Morton, Jelly Roll, 88
Movies, 98–100, 117
Murderers' Row, 109
Music, 87–89, 90, 95, 102
Musical hits, 1919–1929, 89
Mussolini, Benito, 48

Nanook of the North, 100
National Aeronautics and Space Administration, 84
National American Woman Suffrage Association (NAWSA), 22, 23
National Broadcasting Company (NBC), 81
National City Bank, 64
National Football League (NFL), 111
National Geographic magazine, 94
National Guard, 31
National Hockey League, 113
Nationalist party (Guomindang), 54
National Organization for Women, 24
National Origins Acts (1921, 1924), 32
National Prohibition Act (1920), 26
National Socialist (Nazi) party, 48
National Woman's Party (NWP), 22, 23
Native Americans, vote and, 23
Negri, Pola, 100
Negro baseball leagues, 110
Negro World, 18
New Economic Policy (NEP), 42–43
New Negro, The, 90
New Orleans, 87
New Orleans Rhythm Kings, 89
News broadcasting, 101
Newspapers, 92–93, 94
 black, 18
Newton, Isaac, 83, 84
New York City, 18
New York *Daily News,* 94
New Yorker magazine, 94, 95
Nicaragua, 56–57
Nicholas II, czar of Russia, 40
Nineteenth Amendment, 23
Ninotchka, 99
Nobel Prize winners, 13, 82, 83, 92
Norge, 79
Norris, Kathleen, 93

North, migration to, 17–19
Northern Expedition, 54
North Pole, 78
Notre Dame, 110–111

Oakley, Annie, 32, 100
O'Keeffe, Georgia, 103
Oliver, Joe "King," 87, 88–89
Olympics, 112, 117
Onassis, Jacqueline Kennedy, 32
O'Neill, Eugene, 96
On the Origin of Species, 85
Organized crime, 26
Original Dixieland Jazz Band, 89
Orlando, Vittorio, 12
Ory, Kid, 88
Oscars, 99–100
Oshimi, General Kenichi, 39
Ottoman Empire, 39, 42, 52
 World War I and, 49–50, 51
Overland Company, 68

Paige, Leroy "Satchel," 110
Palestine, Jewish immigration to, 51, 53
Palestine Problem, 49–53
Paley, William, 81
Palmer, A. Mitchell, 31
Pan-African Conferences, 56
Panama, 56
Paris, 52, 78, 93
Paris Peace Conference, 11–12, 35, 36–37, 51–52
Parker, Dorothy, 16
Paul, Alice, 22
Peary, Robert, 78
Pegler, Westbrook, 105
Penicillin, 82–83
Persia, 52
Petrograd soviets, 40
Petroleum Building, 19
Petroleum industry, 63
Phonofilm, 100
Physics, 83–84
Piano industry, 81
Pickford, Mary, 99–100
Piggly Wiggly, 67
Pilsudski, Joseph, 46
Pittsburgh, 33
Planck, Max, 83
Plane Crazy, 98
Plastic surgery, 82
Poetry, 90, 91, 93–94
Poker Cabinet, 14
Poland, 32, 37, 42, 46
Polio, 13
Pollution Act (1924), 16
Pound, Ezra, 93–94
Pravda, 44
Presidential elections, 13–14, 16, 23, 57, 80
Prices, 45–46, *59,* 60, 64, 65, 71
Progressivism, 22, 25
Prohibition, 24–29
Puerto Rico, 32
Pulitzer Prize winners, 93, 96
Pullman Company, 61
Purges, 44

Quantum mechanics, 83–84
Queen Christina, 99

Race relations, 17, *17.* See also African-Americans
 Ku Klux Klan and, 31–33
Radio, 16, 79–81, *87,* 95, 97, 101–102
Radio City Music Hall, 103
Radio Corporation of America (RCA), 79, 81
Rainey, Gertrude "Ma," 89
Randolph, Asa Philip, 61
Reader's Digest, 94, 95
Real Folks, 101
Recession, 59
Recreation, *105*
Red Russians, 42
Red Scare, 30–31, 61
Religion, 85, 97
Reza Shah Pahlavi, 52
Rhapsody in Blue, 89
Rice, Grantland, 105, 110, 111, 114
Roads, 70, *70*
Roaring Twenties, 60
Robeson, Paul, 90
Robinson, Jackie, 110
Rockets, 79
Rockne, Knute, 110–111
Rogers, Will, 16, 67, 95
Roosevelt, Eleanor, 13
Roosevelt, Franklin Delano, 13, 57, 61
 affliction with polio, 13
Roosevelt, Theodore, 32
Rose Bowl, 81
Ross, Harold, 95
Ross, Nellie Tayloe, 24
Rowlatt Acts, 54
Runyon, Damon, 105
Russia. *See also* Union of Soviet Socialist Republics
 civil war in, 41, 42
 economy of, 45
 revolutions in, 40–42
 World War I and, 36, 40
Ruth, George Herman "Babe," 105, 108–109, 110, 116

Sacco, Nicola, 31
Safety Last, 98
Sandino, General César Augusto, 56–57
Sarazen, Gene, 114
Sarnoff, David, 79, 81
Saturday Evening Post, 94, 106
Saudi Arabia, 52
Schulz, Charles M., 100
Scopes, John, 85
Scopes trial, 84–85
Sears and Roebuck, 67
Seeing Eye, Inc., The, 73
Sèvres, Treaty of, 51
Shangdong province, 53–54
Sharecroppers, 21
Shaw, George Bernard, 105, 112
Sheik, The, 100
Sheppard, Morris, 27
Sherlock Junior, 99

Show Boat, 96
Shuffle Along, 89
Silent films, 99
Simmons, "Colonel" William J., 32
Simon and Schuster, 106
Sinn Fein, 47
Skyscrapers, 19
Sloan, Alfred P., 69
Smith, Alfred K., 16
Smith, Bessie, 89
Smith, "Moe," 28–29
Socialism, 43
Socialist Democratic Labor party (Russian), 41, 44
Solvay Congress, 83
Son of the Sheik, The, 100
Souls of Black Folk, The, 90
Sound and the Fury, The, 93
South, immigration from, 17–19
South Pole, 79
Sparrows, 100
Speakeasies, 27–28, 29, 89
Speculation, in stock market, 72–73
Spirit of St. Louis, 78
Sports, 105–106, 107–117
  African-Americans in, 110, 112
  women in, 113, 114, 115, 117
Sports journalism, 105–106
Stalin, Joseph (Joseph Dzugashvili), 43–44
Standard Oil of New Jersey, 67
Stanley Cup, 113
Stanton, Elizabeth Cady, 22
Steamboat Willie, 98
Steel industry, 61
Stein, Gertrude, 93
Stieglitz, Alfred, 103
Stock market, 60, 63–64, 72
  crash of 1929, 72, 73
  Great Depression and, 72–73
Stop Flirting, 95
Stores, 67
Stout Air Lines, 77
Strikes, 30, 60
  in Britain, 46
Suburbs, 19, 70
Suez Canal, 52
Sun Also Rises, The, 93
Sunday, Billy, 97

Sunshine Hour, The, 97
Sun Yixian (Sun Yat-sen), 54
Supermarkets, 67
Swanson, Gloria, 100
Swimming, 117
Sykes-Picot Agreement, 50
Syria, 53

Tabloid newspapers, 94
Talkies, 99
Tarzan Escapes, 117
Tarzan the Ape Man, 117
Teapot Dome scandal, 14–15
Technology, 63, 71
Temperance movement, 24–26
Temple Mount, 53
Ten Commandments, The, 100
Tennessee, 84–85
Tennis, 113–114
Terminal Tower, 19
Thief of Bagdad, The, 100
This Side of Paradise, 92
Thomas, Lowell, 101
Thorpe, Jim, 111
Three Ages, The, 99
Tilden, William Tatem "Big Bill," 113–114
Time magazine, 94, 95
Titanic, 79
Tokyo, 53
Tournament of Roses parade, 96
Trade, international, 46, 56
Transjordan, 53
Transportation, 67–70, 77–79. *See also* Aircraft; Automobile industry
Treaty of Brest-Litovsk, 42, 43
Treaty of Sèvres, 51
Treaty of Versailles, 37, 38, 45, 46, 48
Tribune Tower, 19
Trotsky, Leon, 40, 42, 43
True Story magazine, 94
Tunney, Gene, 112–113
Turkey, 51. *See also* Ottoman Empire
Tutankhamen's tomb, 81

Ukraine, 42
Ulysses, 94
Uncertainty principle, 83

Unemployment, 22
  in Germany, *35*
Union Cigar, 73
Union of Soviet Socialist Republics (USSR), 40–44. *See also* Russia
Unions. *See* Labor movement
U.S. mail, 77
U.S. Steel, 62
United Universal Negro Improvement Association (UNIA), 18
Urbanization, 19–20, *20*, 29, 67–68

Valentino, Rudolph, 100, 106
Vallee, Rudy, 102
Vanzetti, Bartolomeo, 31
Versailles, Treaty of, 37, 45, 46, 48
Victor Emmanuel III, king of Italy, 48
Vogue magazine, 94
Volstead Act (1920), 26
Vote. *See also* Elections
  African-Americans and, 22
  Native Americans and, 23
  women and, 22–24

Wages, 17, 22, 60, 64, 76, 110
Wailing Wall, 53
Wallace, DeWitt, 95
Wallace, Lila, 95
Walt Disney Productions, 98
War Communism, 42–43
War Industries Board, 59–60
War reparations, 12, 36, 37, 45, 48
Washington, D.C., 18
Washington Conference, 39–40
Waste Land, The, 94
WEAF, 80
Weary Blues, The, 91
Weimar Republic, 48
Weiss, Ehrich (Harry Houdini), 100
Weissmuller, Johnny, 117
Weizmann, Dr. Chaim, 50–51, 52
Westinghouse Electric Company, 79
Wharton, Edith, 93

White, G. H., 31–33
"White City, The," 91
White-collar workers, 19–20, 60
Whiteman, Paul, 102
White Russians, 42
Whitney, Casper W., 111
Willard, Jess, 112
Wills, Helen, 113, 114
Wilson, Woodrow, 23, 32
  economy and, 59
  Fourteen Points of, 35–36
  Paris Peace Conference and, 11–12, 35, 36
  Treaty of Versailles and, 37, 38
Wings, 99–100
Wolverines, 89
Women, 29
  employment of, 22–23, 62
  in politics, 24
  in sports, 113, 114, 115, 117
  suffrage and, 22–24
  World War I and, 22–23
Women's Christian Temperance Union, 25
Women's movement, 22–24
Wood, Grant, 102
Woodbury's Facial Soap, 66
Woolworth, 67
Workweek, 76
World Court, 38
World Series, 107, 109
World War I
  Africa and, 55
  economy and, 59, 64
  Europe after, 44–49
  Middle East and, 49–53, *50*
  Paris Peace Conference and, 11–12, 35, 36–37, 51–52
  Treaty of Versailles and, 37, 45, 46, 48
  women and, 22–23
World Zionist Congress, 50
Wright, Frank Lloyd, 103

Yellow Cab Company, 70
Yellow Drive-It-Yourself System, Inc., 70
Yugoslavia, 37

Ziegfeld *Follies,* 95–96
Zionism, 50, 52